Derwent Valley Walks

Derwent Valley **Walks**

Discover the Derwent Valley and World Heritage Site

Walks and Features

DENIS EARDLEY

Acknowledgements

I would like to thank Gillian Eardley, John Hollinshead and Adrian Farmer for their invaluable help and encouragement in compiling this book.

First published in Great Britain in 2011 by The Derby Books Publishing Company Limited, 3 The Parker Centre, Derby, DE21 4SZ.

ISBN 978-1-85983-960-7

Contents

Introduction

The River Derwent has a truly remarkable tale to tell. Although only 60 miles in length, it fills mighty reservoirs near its source, has been harnessed to power mills and, most importantly, played an outstanding part in the Industrial Revolution. This was recognised in 2001, when the Derwent Valley was awarded World Heritage Status, the site running from Masson Mill at Matlock Bath to the former Derby Silk Mill, a distance of approximately 15 miles. It is the only World Heritage Site in the East Midlands

The Derwent is not a long river, measuring no more than 60 miles from its source to mouth. Rising 2,000ft above sea level, among the rocks and peat of Swains Greave between Bleaklow and Howden Moors near the Yorkshire border, it flows for its full course through Derbyshire. Despite its modest length, it passes through a valley of contrasting landscapes. Wildly beautiful in the north, with majestic man-made dams and reservoirs, it is an area often referred to as the Peak National Park's own Lake District. Further south, as you enter Chatsworth Park, the terrain becomes much more soft and gentle. Later, the river winds its way through the narrow gorge at Matlock, before flowing through meadows and the busy city of Derby on its way to a meeting with the River Trent near Shardlow. One of the best-preserved inland canal ports in the country, it is a fascinating place to explore, still busy with boats, now used for leisure rather than commerce. The boats range from traditional narrow boats with brightly painted liveries, frequently bedecked with pretty flower boxes in summer, to pleasure craft of all shapes and sizes.

Since 1950 the northern half of the Derwent Valley has been part of the Peak District National Park. It was the first National Park to be opened in Great Britain and has been such a success that it is now the second most-visited National Park in the World. Visitors come to the Peak District to find peace, tranquility and adventure, with some of England's finest walking, cycling, climbing and caving readily available. The National Park itself is the home to approximately 38,000 people, and not surprisingly the local economy is heavily based on tourism and farming, with quarrying and manufacturing also playing a part.

Although the southern part of the valley is outside the Peak National Park boundary, visitors are gradually discovering that it has just as much to offer. For hundreds of years the waters from the Derwent have been harnessed to turn grindstones in corn mills and to power hammers for the fulling of cloth and forging of metal. The waters also operated bellows to blast air into furnaces and to drive the frames and mules for spinning cotton.

It was Richard Arkwright, later Sir Richard, who was the driving force behind the Industrial Revolution. He exploited water power to drive his machinery when he moved to Cromford, and he is often referred to as the 'Father of the Factory System'. Further south at Belper, the admirable Strutt's North Mill Visitor Centre tells the story of Jedidiah Strutt and his family, who played a major part in the Industrial Revolution. At Darley Abbey it was the Evans family who contributed substantially to the story, and at Derby the Lombes took on the main role. All this is set in an area of considerable scenic beauty.

There can be no doubt that the Derwent Valley is one of the country's finest assets, both from the point of view of its heritage and its magnificent scenery. The walks and features in this book are designed to enable visitors to discover this unique valley. The walks can be completed in short or long stages, dependent on time and choice. Refreshment stops and places of interest in the locality are also listed.

The Walks

Linear walks are great fun as long as you do a little planning in advance and obtain bus or train timetable information. You can choose how many stages of the walk you want to do before returning to the starting point. The Derwent Valley is well served by buses, and many of the walks also have the benefit of train services.

This book contains 20 linear walks, which guide you along the Derwent Valley from Fairholmes in the north to Derwent Mouth in the south, close to the borders of Nottinghamshire and Leicestershire. There are 10 circular walks, which can all be subdivided into two shorter walks, which enables you to explore much of the dramatic scenery that surrounds the valley at your own pace.

Although many of the linear walks are comparatively easy to follow, it is always advisable to carry an Ordnance Survey Map. This is particularly the case for the circular walks, which are much more detailed.

It is very important to wear appropriate footwear and clothing, as even on the brightest of days the weather may change and the ground underfoot may be unexpectedly wet and muddy. Consulting the local weather forecast in advance will give you a good idea of what to take with you when you set out on a walk.

Suggested refreshment stops, suitable for both linear and circular walks, have been listed. It is advisable to check in advance the times that food is served to avoid disappointment, particularly where the choice of alternative establishments is limited.

There are numerous places of interest, both in the Derwent Valley and a little further away, which, if you have the time, you will find well worth the effort of visiting. Some are open all year, others on a more restricted basis. You will find suggested lists with the circular walks.

General information about the Derwent Valley and its attractions, as well as guidance on where to stay, is available from numerous sources, including the following:

Castleton Visitor Centre (Tel. 01433 620679) – Upper Derwent
Chesterfield Tourist Information Centre (Tel. 01246 345777/8) – North Eastern Derwent
Bakewell Information Centre (Tel. 01629 816558) – Central Derwent
Matlock Tourist Information Centre (Tel. 01629 583388) – Central Derwent
Derby Tourist Information Centre (Tel. 01332 255802) – Southern Derwent

Important Notes

Walking

All the walks in this book have been carefully checked and should provide visitors with a great deal of pleasure, subject to careful planning in advance. There are 20 linear walks, where you can easily choose to walk one or more stages. All 10 circular walks have been subdivided into shorter walks, giving you the option of a further 30 walks.

The contents of this book have been very carefully checked and are believed to be correct at the date of publication. The author cannot be held responsible for any errors and omissions, however, or for changes in the detail given that occur due to diversion orders and permissions being withdrawn, or for any other reason. Participation is at the walker's own risk. The maps contained within this publication are intended only as a general guide and are not to scale. If any reader finds that significant changes have been made to any route, it will be appreciated if they make contact with the publisher.

Walking can be strenuous, and it is up to the individual to assess their own level of fitness. All the walks described should not present difficulties to a moderately fit person carrying appropriate clothing, equipment and maps. Care should always be taken to supervise children and animals carefully, both in the country and on the roads.

On many of the walks a considerable number of stiles are encountered, which may present problems to some people, including dog owners. The time taken to complete each individual walk varies, dependent on fitness and the number of stops.

Car Parking

Many of the car parks suggested are public, so remember to take plenty of loose change with you. When you have to park by the roadside or in a lay-by, please ensure that you park safely and without inconveniencing others. Beware of thieves, do not leave any items of value clearly visible in the car and ensure that you leave the car securely locked. Pub car parks should not be used unless you have the owner's permission.

Public Transport

All the walks listed in this book start and finish at points where public transport is easily accessible. For further information, please telephone 0871 200 2233 or visit: www.travelineeastmidlands.org.uk. Plan in advance and give yourself plenty of time to reach the appointed pick-up point.

Refreshment Stops

Opening times at pubs and tea shops frequently vary according to the time of the year – last-minute changes are not uncommon. In case of uncertainty, especially where there are no other suitable alternatives, it is best to telephone in advance, particularly if food is required.

1
Lost Villages and the Construction of the Reservoirs – Tip's Tale

The Howden, Derwent and Ladybower reservoirs in the Upper Derwent Valley at the heart of the Peak National Park make up an area often referred to as the 'Lake District of the Peak'. The reservoirs are surrounded by magnificent countryside where water and woodland, topped by high moors, predominate. In recent years forestry has become an important factor and the sides of the valley have been clothed in conifers.

Not surprisingly, the area has become so popular that it acts as a magnet for walkers, cyclists, fell-runners and people who just come to relax and enjoy the outstanding beauty of the countryside. At certain times the road beyond Fairholmes is closed to help protect the environment and a mini-bus service is operated. Disabled Badge holders are exempt.

The Upper Derwent Information Centre is based at Fairholmes and provides facilities for visitors. Bikes can be hired, maps and books can be bought and general information about the area can be obtained from the rangers. There are also large car parks, toilets and plenty of room for picnics.

Prior to the 20th century the valley was home to a thriving farming community with two ancient hamlets: Derwent, with its Jacobean hall, and Ashopton. The Upper Derwent valley was a very attractive location for the storage of water, with its long, deep valley and narrow points for dam building.

This, combined with a high average rainfall, low population level and heavy demand for water from the industrial towns that surrounded the Peak District, made the case for reservoir construction. The Derwent Valley Water Board was set up in 1899 to supply water to Derby, Nottingham, Sheffield and Leicester, and the Howden and Derwent Reservoirs were constructed in the early 1900s.

The Howden and Derwent Reservoirs were built in the upper reaches of the valley and, with the exception of a few isolated farmhouses, the flooding did not create extensive disruption. Both the Howden and Derwent were completed by 1916. The 1.25 million tons of stones used in construction was transported to the site by rail on a specially constructed narrow-gauge line from Bamford.

During the building of the two reservoirs, over 1,000 navvies and their families lived in a temporary village known as Birchinlee, or 'Tin Town' because the living quarters were made of corrugated iron. It was situated by the present road alongside Howden Reservoir, and for a decade at the beginning of the 20th century it was a self-sufficient community.

Birchinlee's infrastructure included a hospital, a school, a canteen, a post office, shops, a recreation hall, a public bathhouse, a police station, a railway station and a rubbish dump with an incinerator. Accommodation comprised of workmen's huts, foremen's huts and married workmen's huts. The latter were decorated to a high standard, as photographs from the period confirm. All that now remains are a few grassed-over foundations and terraces on which the houses stood. The former railway track has been converted into a footpath.

Gwinnett House, where Miss A. Cotterill remained after the flooding of the Ladybower Reservoir.

Following the construction of the two reservoirs, the demand for water was satisfied, and although plans existed for further reservoirs, no further action was taken. But demand continued to grow and the decision was taken to build one very large reservoir, to be called Ladybower. This entailed the flooding of the villages of Ashopton and Derwent and caused considerable unrest.

The project went ahead, however, and the tiny village of Yorkshire Bridge was built to accommodate those rendered homeless by the flooding of the valley. The village lies in the shadow of the dam wall of the Ladybower Reservoir, with its houses in neat, regimented rows. One person, however, refused to move: Miss A. Cotterill of Gwinnett House. She remained there until she died in 1990 at the age of 99, the waters of the reservoir lapping at the front garden steps.

Yorkshire Bridge has its own pub of the same name and the bridge spanning the River Derwent also bears the same name. Despite all the references to Yorkshire, you are still in Derbyshire; the boundary between the two counties is more than two

Yorkshire Bridge, where the inhabitants of Derwent and Ashopton were rehoused.

Ladybower Lodge residential accommodation, formerly Water Board Offices.

miles away to the north-east. The visitor centre at Fairholmes, situated further north, below the wall of the Derwent Dam, tells the story of the 'drowned villages' and the birth of Yorkshire Bridge.

The packhorse bridge that stood near to the gates of Derwent Hall had a preservation order on it. It was moved stone by stone and rebuilt sometime later at Slippery Stones at the head of the Howden Reservoir. All the graves in the churchyard were excavated and the bodies reburied in nearby Bamford churchyard.

A few properties built on slightly higher land, including the Shooting Lodge and former Roman Catholic School, survived. But the majority were demolished and flooded, leaving the church spire eerily poking out above the waters, before eventually being blown up.

Ashopton Viaduct was built to carry the Snake Road to Glossop, and the Ladybower Viaduct was built to carry the road from Yorkshire Bridge to the A57. In 1945 the flooding was completed, and the

Derwent Dam Wall and North Tower.

The Shooting Lodge still remains after the flooding of the valley.

opening ceremony was carried out on Tuesday 25 September 1945 by King George VI.

During periods of severe drought, hundreds of visitors have been able to walk on the roads of the 'lost villages', identified by the remains of stone walls standing on the parched bottom of the reservoir. The railway line used in the construction of Howden and Derwent Reservoirs was reopened as a timberline when Ladybower was built. It was purchased by the Peak District National Park Authority in 1944, and is now a bridleway and footpath.

The Derwent Dams were used during World War Two by the 617 Dambusters Squadron of Lancaster Bombers to perfect the 'bouncing bombs' technique, which in 1943 breached the Ruhr Valley Dams in the heartland of industrial Germany. The area was chosen because of the similarity to the Möhne and Eder Dams. A plaque and a memorial museum in the west tower of Derwent Dam retells the story of the Dambusters. The museum is open most Sundays and Bank Holidays throughout the year.

Together the three reservoirs form the largest area of open water in Derbyshire and the Peak District National Park, and have a combined capacity of 463,692 million litres. Following the

Looking out over Derwent Reservoir.

Farm at Derwent that escaped the flooding of the valley.

passing of Water Acts in 1973 and 1974, the Derwent Valley Water Board's reservoirs and land were transferred to the newly formed Severn Trent Water Authority, the second largest water board in the country. As a result of a further Water Act in 1989, the water industry was privatised and Severn Trent Water became a private company. A clause in the act ensures that land owned by the water company cannot be sold off without consultation with the Countryside Commission.

Tip's Tale

Perhaps the best known inhabitant to have lived at Yorkshire Bridge was a sheepdog named Tip. Her master, Joseph Tagg, served for many years as a shepherd for the 15th Duke of Norfolk. Tagg was a well-known local character, called 'Old Joe' by his friends, who lived with his niece at Yorkshire Bridge during his later years. He helped found Hope Valley Sheepdog Trials and gained a reputation as a sheepdog breeder.

He remained active in later life and, on Saturday 12 December 1953, at the age of 85, he went out with his faithful Border collie, Tip, to tend some sheep. By the following day the alarm was raised and a RAF Mountain Rescue team, gamekeepers and shepherds set up a search. Despite all their efforts, no trace of the two could be found.

It was not until Saturday 27 March 1954, exactly 15 weeks later, that they were found by two men from the water board, who were rounding up sheep high on Ronksley Moor. Tagg's remains were discovered in a slight depression in the ground. His faithful dog, Tip, now completely exhausted, was lying on guard about five yards away. Somehow, Tip had managed to

Fairholmes Visitor Centre at the north end of Ladybower Reservoir.

survive for 105 days throughout heavy snow, biting winds and freezing temperatures on one of the most hostile stretches of moorland in the country.

Tip was carried back to the rescuer's lorry and later returned to the caring home of Tagg's niece, where she was carefully nursed back to health. Once the story became known, Tip became famous not only in this country, but abroad as well. The loyal dog was presented with the Bronze Medal of the Canine Defence League – the equivalent of the Victoria Cross in the animal world.

Sadly, Tip died the following year on 16 February, and when the news spread the hearts of those that had heard the story were so greatly touched that donations for a memorial were received from all over the world. The memorial was erected at the western end of Derwent Dam and Tip's remains were buried on the moors where she had been found near her deceased master.

Tip's Memorial by the side of Derwent Dam (Tip's Tale).

2
Fairholmes to Heatherdene

The Walk

This outstanding walk starts at the Upper Derwent Information Centre based at Fairholmes, which overlooks Ladybower Reservoir and is surrounded by forest, farmland and wild, glorious moorland scenery. Ladybower is the largest and most recently constructed of the three reservoirs, which make up the National Park's 'Lake District'. It was constructed by flooding the villages of Ashopton and Derwent and the rehousing of the inhabitants.

The Upper Derwent Valley was first used as a summer hunting ground for early man. After the Norman Conquest of 1066 the valley became part of the Royal Forest of the Peak and was used as a hunting reserve. An ancient bridleway ran through the valley from Derwent to Glossop and was used by trains of packhorses transporting goods across the Peak District.

The Derwent Dams were used during World War Two to perfect the 'bouncing bombs' technique, which in 1943 breached the Ruhr Valley Dams in the heartland of industrial Germany. The memorial museum in the west tower of Derwent Dam retells the story of the Dambusters.

All that remains of the former Derwent village, after it was flooded to make way for the reservoir, are a few houses and other buildings, which are passed near the start of the walk. In

Ladybower Viaduct.

Ladybower Inn on the A57 near Ladybower Viaduct.

addition, there are a number of hill farms scattered about the area, most involved in sheep farming. The hardy white-faced woodland sheep are often seen in this part of the Peak National Park.

Derwent Hall in the village of Derwent was one of the casualties of flooding. It was built in 1672 by the Belguy family and later owned by the Duke of Norfolk, before becoming a well-known youth hostel in 1931.

Leaving the banks of the reservoir behind, the route climbs up through what remains of Ashopton, before taking a path across moorland and through Ladybower Wood, a Derbyshire Wildlife Trust Nature Reserve noted for its ancient woodland.

Ashopton Viaduct was built to carry the Snake Road to Glossop, and the Ladybower Viaduct was built to carry the road from Yorkshire Bridge to the A57. The reservoir was finally opened by King George VI in 1945 and, to mark the occasion, a commemorative monument has been built close to the dam wall.

The tiny village of Yorkshire Bridge lies in the shadow of the dam wall of the Ladybower Reservoir. Its neat, regimented rows of houses were built to rehouse the inhabitants of the former villages of Ashopton and Derwent when their homes were submerged.

Finger Post Sign for Cutthroat Bridge, pointing the way over the moor.

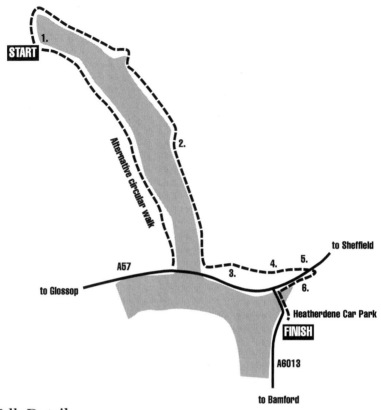

Walk Details

Length: 4 miles, or 7 miles if circular walk is undertaken.

Start/Finish: Fairholmes (SK172892) – Heatherdene car park.

Starting Walk: Fairholmes Visitor Centre, at the north end of Ladybower Reservoir, off the A57 Glossop to Sheffield road. Car park available with overflow facilities, but can be very busy during peak holiday periods. Check timetable for bus service.

Finishing Walk: There are a number of options available. 1) If you wish to continue at the end of this walk, go to the Heatherdene to Bamford route section. 2) If you wish to walk back to Fairholmes, follow the instructions in the note below. 3) To return to Fairholmes by bus, there is a stop on the other side of the road to the Ladybower Inn. Also, buses stop at Fearfall Wood (turning circle), which is on the opposite side of the reservoir, a short distance up the road leading to Fairholmes. Buses run more frequently on summer weekends and Bank Holiday Mondays. 4) Buses stop in both directions close to the turn-off for Heatherdene Car Park.

Walker on the path round Ladybower.

Terrain: Easy, mainly level walking among beautiful moorland scenery. The walk takes you along good paths down the eastern side of Ladybower Reservoir, before a short climb up and over moorland countryside and through Ladybower Wood to join the A57.

The path across moorland leading to Ladybower Wood, with distant views of the reservoir.

Ahead is the path along the northern side of Ladybower Reservoir.

The Route

1. From the Visitor Centre, follow the footpath round to the right; this soon joins the road in front of the towering Derwent Dam wall. Continue along the road as it bends to the right, taking you through what remains of the old Derwent village.

2. Stay on the track by the reservoir without deviating, until just as you are approaching the A57. After passing through a stile, go to the left, past a sign for Cutthroat Bridge, to ascend a road up through what remains of Ashopton.

3. Shortly after passing Ding Bank Farm, where the path divides, go right at a gateway signed for Cutthroat Bridge.

4. Follow the rough path along the bracken-clad hillside with the wall close on your right.

5. Enter Ladybower Wood through a stile, and follow the obvious path passing above the Ladybower Inn, before turning sharp right to descend for 100 yards to the side of the public house.

6. Turn right down the A57* and walk in front of the pub (buses for Fairholmes stop here – limited service), turn left at the intersection with the A6013 and cross the Ladybower Viaduct. Heatherdene car park is on the left as you approach the dam wall at the southern end of the reservoir.

*Note: If you wish to make the walk circular, continue on the A57 until you have crossed Ashopton Viaduct, and turn right towards Fairholmes. After a few yards, go through the stile on the right and follow the surfaced path back towards the Upper Derwent Visitor Centre. Shortly before reaching Fairholmes, the path joins the road running up the Derwent Valley at a small roadside car park. Follow the road for a short distance, before turning down an obvious path that leads you to the top corner of Fairholmes car park (3 miles).

3
Heatherdene to Bamford

The Walk

This lovely walk starts at the southern end of the Peak National Park's 'Lake District', at Heatherdene car park and picnic site, situated in one of the most picturesque spots in the county. The walk along the tree-lined path from the car park is particularly striking on a sunny day, with the waters of the Ladybower Reservoir twinkling in the sunshine through the trees.

Following the renovation of the Ladybower Dam, a permissive path has been opened across the dam wall. At the western end of the dam is a small sculpture that forms part of the Bamford Touchstones Sculpture Trail, established by the residents of Bamford to mark the millennium. The Touchstones illustrate Air, Water, Earth and Fire and are situated on a five-mile walk around the edges

The Derwent Valley Heritage Way starts at Heatherdene.

Interesting carved seat at Heatherdene Car Park.

View across Ladybower Dam from Heatherdene.

of the village. A central Touchstone combines all four elements and a Celtic symbol is present on all the touchstones to signify the millennium. A pamphlet with maps and a description of the trail can be found at various outlets in the village.

The path soon joins the Thornhill Trail, which runs along a former railway line. It is made up of a mixture of grass and compacted stone. The line was specially constructed to carry stone from the railway sidings at Bamford to Fairholmes when the Derwent and Howden Dams were constructed during the early 1900s. In the 1930s, when Ladybower was built, it was reopened as a timberline. When it no longer served any useful purpose it was purchased by the Peak District National Park Authority and is now a bridleway and footpath.

The superbly situated village of Bamford stands at the heart of the Dark Peak, below Bamford Edge and close to the Ladybower Reservoir and the Upper Derwent Valley Dams. It is the sole

Ladybower Reservoir pumping stations.

This Millennium Touchstone is situated by the reservoir dam and is part of a five-mile trail.

surviving village in the Peak National Park's 'Lake District'; the villages of Ashopton and Derwent were submerged when the Ladybower Reservoir was constructed.

In an area so dominated by hills, with few fences in evidence and sheep in the majority, it might be thought that the Industrial Revolution had not had much of an effect. This is not the case, as a corn mill operated at Bamford in the first half of the 18th century, and then switched to spinning cotton, before the mill burnt down.

The Moore family rebuilt the mill, created a weir to provide more power to their cotton mill and gradually recruited a substantial workforce. Having changed hands several times, it closed as a cotton mill in 1965. For a time the mill was used to make small electrical furnaces, but it has now been converted into accommodation.

Near the end of the walk, the local Quakers' Meeting House and gardens are passed on Water Lane. There is a car park for the community and visitors further along the lane, after you pass the gateway to the house. There are about 28,000 members and attenders of the Religious Society of Friends in Britain.

Bamford Railway Station, to the south of the village, is a popular stopping point on the Hope Valley line that links Sheffield to Manchester. On the road just below the station the Peak Park has re-erected the Mytham Bridge Toll Gate, which used to stand nearby. This was one of the toll gates on the first turnpike road in the area – built in 1758 to link Sheffield to Sparrowpit. There is also an 18-hole golf course at Sickleholme, near the station.

Thornhill Trail was formerly a railway line that served the building of the reservoirs.

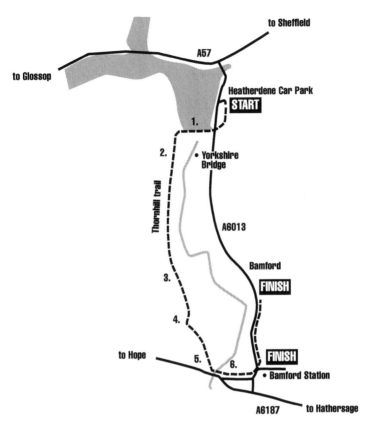

Walk Details

Length: 2.5 miles.

Start/Finish: Heatherdene car park (SK202858) – Bamford Railway Station/Bamford Village centre.

Starting Walk: The Severn Trent car park at Heatherdene is situated on the A6013, approximately a quarter of a mile from the intersection with the A57 Glossop to Sheffield road. Buses stop in both directions close to the turn-off for Heatherdene car park.

Finishing Walk: The bus stop for both directions is located by the turning circle at the former Mytham Bridge Toll Gate on the A6013; the railway station is on the opposite side of the road. Bus stops are also available at the centre of Bamford.

Terrain: An easy, mostly level route full of variety, with excellent views of Ladybower Reservoir in the early stages, followed by a walk along a converted railway track through woodland.

Dog walker on the Thornhill Trail, a former railway line.

The Route

1. Leave the car park through the picnic area and follow the path to the A6013, cross the road and use the concessionary path to walk along the dam wall to the southern end of Ladybower Reservoir, then turn left down an access road.

2. Follow the road down, and after almost 300 yards turn right at a fingerpost sign marked 'Thornhill Trail'; a railway line that has been converted for leisure purposes.

3. Continue along an obvious path, cross the Thornhill to Yorkshire Bridge road at a zigzag, which first bends to the left and then back again, to revert to the same direction that you were walking in before.

4. On reaching Water Lane, turn left. After 75 yards, with the Quaker Community Centre on the opposite side of the lane, cross a stile on your right into a field, by a footpath sign for Shatton.

Farm close to the Thornhill Trail, with the the A6013 in the background.

Derwent Water Board House, which is now used by the Quakers.

5. Keep close to the hedge, follow the field round and go through a stile. Turn right and walk under a railway bridge, which leads you to a gravel path at the top of the High Peak Garden Centre car park.

6. Walk forward to the A6187 (to continue the walk to the next section, cross the road and follow the Bamford to Hathersage route instructions), turn left, walk past the garden centre, cross the bridge and immediately turn left to walk up a cul-de-sac. At the top of the cul-de-sac is Mytham Bridge Toll Gate on the A6013, where the bus stop is situated, with the railway station across the road. The village centre is about half a mile away to the north.

Sign for Shatton, with the Quaker Community Gardens in the background.

4
Fairholmes to Bamford Circular Walk

The Walk

An outstanding walk in the Upper Derwent Valley, which starts at Fairholmes Visitor Centre, located near to Derwent Dam. It is the starting point for several circular walks. Here information is available in a number of formats, including books, leaflets and guides.

The northbound road past Fairholmes is not open at peak times. There is a shuttle bus service available when the road is closed, however. From Fairholmes the road continues for approximately five miles. After that, a bridleway runs along the other side of the reservoir.

The carved pole at Fairholmes Visitor Centre, at the northern end of Ladybower Reservoir.

View of one of several farms in the Upper Derwent Valley.

Ashopton Viaduct as seen looking through the trees near Heatherdene Car Park

The Derwent Dams were used as flying practice for very low-level bomb aiming techniques by the 617 RAF Squadron during World War Two. On 16 May 1943, 19 Lancaster bombers, powered by four Rolls-Royce Merlin engines, took off in waves from RAF Scampton, each heavily loaded with just one revolving bouncing bomb each. The squadron suffered heavy losses, but were successful in their mission, the bombing producing heavy floods and badly damaging German production in the Ruhr.

Water has been stored for centuries in the Peak District by damming streams to create man-made reservoirs. Dams were also built to provide the power to drive mill wheels. The biggest and most famous reservoirs in the Peak District are in the Upper Derwent Valley. Howden, Derwent and Ladybower Reservoirs provide drinking water for the towns and cities that surround the area, including Sheffield, Derby, Leicester and Nottingham.

The drowning of the villages of Ashopton and Derwent to create the Ladybower caused great distress among the people who had to vacate their homes. Initially, Derwent Church was demolished, but not the spire. A touching

Bamford Edge towers above the valley on the easten side.

Despite the name, the Yorkshire Bridge Inn is in Derbyshire.

reminder of the submerged villages occurred for many years afterwards when the spire reappeared during times of drought. During a particularly dry summer in 1959 hundreds of visitors revisited Derwent village. After that summer the water board had the spire demolished for safety reasons.

From Yorkshire Bridge Hotel, New Road climbs steadily up along the flanks of Bamford Edge, with extensive views of the Hope Valley and down to Bamford. The stone used in the construction of the weir at the mill in the village came from the moor.

The superbly situated village of Bamford stands below Bamford Edge. It is the sole surviving village in Derbyshire's 'Lake District'. Opposite the triangle of land at the centre of the village is what must be one of the most picturesque post offices in the county, with its bay window and leaded panes and comfortable seat outside the door. It was once Bamford's oldest public house,

the Cheshire Cheese.

Thornhill Trail, a converted railway line, provides a peaceful woodland walk before Ladybower Reservoir is reached.

Queen Victoria's Diamond Jubilee Stone 1897, by the roadside at the centre of Bamford.

Bamford Mill, now used for accommodation purposes.

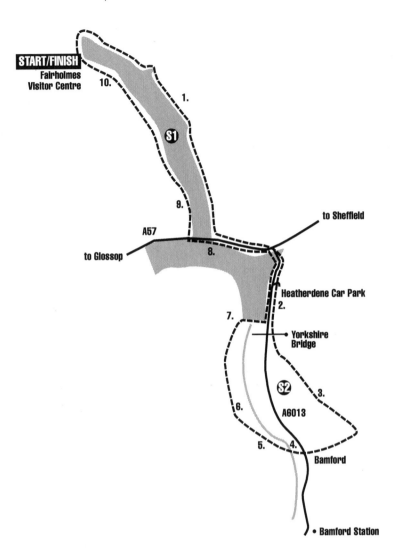

Walk Details

Length: 10.5 miles (Short Walk I – 5.75 miles, Short Walk II – 4.5 miles).

Start/Finish: Fairholmes car park (SK172892).

Starting/Finishing Walk: Fairholmes Visitor Centre is situated at the north end of Ladybower Reservoir, off the A57 Glossop to Sheffield road. A car park is available with overflow facilities, but it can be very busy during peak holiday periods. Buses stop in both directions close to the turn-off for Heatherdene car park. To start the walk, railway users should make their way up the A6013 to the centre of Bamford and follow the instructions from Point 4 onwards, leaving the walk at Point 3.

Terrain: Mainly level walking among beautiful moorland scenery, but with a steady ascent towards Bamford Edge, followed by a steep descent. The early stages of the walk takes you along good paths down the eastern side of Ladybower Reservoir. The return journey along the Thornhill Trail and the western side of Ladybower is relatively flat and easy.

The Route

1. From the Visitor Centre follow the footpath round to the right. After a short distance it joins the road, which runs in front of the towering Derwent Dam wall. Follow the road as it bends to the right, taking you through what remains of the old Derwent village. Stay on the road, which later turns into a footpath, by the side of the reservoir without deviating until you reach the A57.

2. Here you turn left and follow the A57 to its intersection with the A6013, where you turn right and cross the Ladybower Viaduct. Continue along the footpath, past the entrance to Heatherdene car park. Soon afterwards the Yorkshire Bridge Hotel is passed.

3. A few yards further on, turn left up New Road, which steadily climbs towards Bamford Edge. When the road levels out and starts to bend to the left, you turn right at a fingerpost sign. The route descends steeply along a partly surfaced track, before eventually arriving at the outskirts of Bamford. Maintain the same direction through the village to arrive in the centre of Bamford by a triangular piece of land.

4. Cross the A6013 and continue ahead down a narrow access road named The Hollow. Turn right near the bottom of the road into a private car park, where, about two thirds of the way down, you turn left at a footpath sign. Walk past Bamford Mill, now turned into flats. Cross the river by an unusual combination of stepping stones and two high footbridges to reach a field on the other side.

Unusual footbridge at Bamford Mill, a combination of stepping stones and two high footbridges.

31

Visitors admiring the view from
the path on the western side of
Ladybower.

5. Head diagonally across the field
   to a stile in the corner, continue
   in the same direction across the
   next field to a stile by a gate.
   Walk down a cart track to the
   left of a barn to go over a stile
   into the next field. Turn left by
   a footpath sign and walk up the
   field, close to the hedge on your
   left. Part way up the field, go
   over a stile on your left, and
   after about 15 yards turn right
   along a former railway line
   track, which has been made
   available to walkers.

6. The track soon crosses the
   Thornhill to Yorkshire Bridge
   road, before continuing through woodland to reach an access road.

7. Continue up the access road for about 300 yards. Opposite a Bamford Touchstones
   Sculpture Trail exhibit, turn right and walk along a concessionary path, provided by
   Severn Trent Water Authority, across the dam wall of the Ladybower Reservoir. On
   reaching the other side, turn left down the A6013 to walk past Heatherdene car park on
   your right.

8. Continue in the same direction, crossing the Ladybower Viaduct to arrive at a T-junction
   of roads. Here you go to the left along the A57 Sheffield to Glossop road and across the
   Ashopton Viaduct.

9. As soon as you are over the viaduct, take the road on the right leading to Fairholmes and
   the Derwent and Howden Reservoirs. After a few yards go through a stile on the right
   and follow the clearly marked permissive path, which runs between the road to your left
   and the reservoir to your right.

10. Shortly before reaching Fairholmes, the path joins the road running up the Derwent
    Valley at a small roadside car park. Follow the road to the right for a short distance,
    before turning down an obvious path that leads you to the top corner of Fairholmes car
    park.

Short Walk I

Ladybower Walk (5.75 miles)
Route (From Fairholmes {SK172892} – A57 – Ashopton Viaduct – Fairholmes)
  1. Follow the Fairholmes to Bamford Circular Route instructions for Point 1.

2. On reaching the A57 Glossop to Sheffield road, turn right and cross the Ashopton Viaduct.
3. As soon as you have crossed the Viaduct, follow the Fairholmes to Bamford Circular Route instructions from Point 9 to Point 10.

Short Walk II

Heatherdene Walk (4.5 miles)

Route (From Heatherdene {SK202858} – Yorkshire Bridge – New Road – Bamford – Thornhill Trail – Heatherdene)

Note: Heatherdene car park is off the A6013 between Yorkshire Bridge and the A57.

1. Leave Heatherdene car park through the picnic area and follow the tree-lined path to the A6013.
2. Turn left to walk up the pavement past the Yorkshire Bridge Hotel.
3. From this point, follow the Fairholmes to Bamford Circular Route instructions from Point 3 to Point 7, taking care to go to the right into Heatherdene car park soon after crossing the dam to the Ladybower Reservoir.

Refreshment Stops

Ladybower Inn (Chapter 2) is located on the A57, at the far-eastern side of Ladybower Reservoir; it was resited over a century ago, having originally been located further up Ladybower Brook. (Tel. 01433 651241)

Upper Derwent Visitor Centre (Chapter 2/4) is located at Fairholmes, close to the Derwent Dam. Drinks and light refreshments are available at the kiosk. Picnic tables are provided outside. (Tel. 01433 650953)

Yorkshire Bridge Inn (Chapter 3/4) overlooks the dam wall of Ladybower Reservoir; it is a large, bustling pub named after a former packhorse bridge. (Tel. 01433 651361)

Anglers Rest (Chapter 3/4) is a small, cosy pub built in 1876, located at the top of the main street in Bamford. (Tel. 01433 651424)

Places of Interest in the Locality

Ladybower and the Derwent Valley is a very popular area for visitors. The dams in the valley were used by Dr Barnes Wallis and his team to test his bouncing bombs, and the film *The Dambusters* was partly shot here.

Upper Derwent Visitor Centre is located at Fairholmes, close to Derwent Dam. Fascinating facts can be found about the area through the interactive displays. Maps, books, postcards, souvenirs, drinks and light refreshments are also available. Picnic tables are provided outside. (Tel. 01433 650953)

Dams and Dambusters Museum is an interesting display, open in the West Tower of Derwent Dam most Sundays and Bank Holidays throughout the year. (Tel. 01433 650953)

Moorland Centre is a new visitor and learning facility, which replaces the former Field Head Centre at Edale. Built at a cost of £1 million, the centre is roofed with sedum turf and heated from the earth and is the UK's first moorland research base. (Tel. 01433 670207)

5
The Villages and Communities of the Upper Derwent – Charlotte Brontë

The northernmost part of the Derwent Valley, where the river rises, is a wild and desolate place, but as the Derwent flows south, sheep farming becomes a viable proposition. A few isolated farms are to be seen sheltering on the hillsides from the biting winds, where snow still regularly falls in the winter.

Little remains of the villages of Derwent and Ashopton, apart from a few high-standing buildings, which were submerged when the Ladybower Reservoir was completed. The residents are now rehoused in the purpose-built village of Yorkshire Bridge, sited close to the reservoir dam wall.

Bamford stands at the heart of the Dark Peak, one and a quarter miles south of Ladybower, with Bamford Edge rising up on the eastern side of the village. It is the sole surviving village in the Peak District National Park's 'Lake District'. Despite the fact that it is at the heart of sheep-rearing country and its most famous event is the annual sheepdog trials, Bamford was once very active in industry.

In the first half of the 18th century a corn mill operated by the Derwent, which was later used for cotton spinning, before being burnt down. The Moore family rebuilt the mill, created

Bamford Village centre.

Bamford Post Office was formerly a public house.

a weir to provide more power to their cotton mill and gradually recruited a substantial workforce. Today the mill is used for accommodation purposes.

By the mill is one of the most fascinating river crossings in the Peak District. It is made up of an unusual combination of stepping stones and two high footbridges, which lead to the field on the other side of the river.

In 1861 William Cameron Moore had the church and vicarage built at his own expense. Both are fine examples of the work of the noted Victorian architect William Butterfield. Before 1860, Anglican services had been held in the National School, built nearly 40 years previously at the same time as the Wesleyan Chapel. Moore also gave generously towards the running of the schools, and the village hall is named after him.

At the centre of the village, in a pleasant green triangle of land, is the Jubilee Stone commemorating Queen Victoria's Jubilee. Opposite the green is an unusual v-shaped stile, with a cut-out designed to allow a bucket of water to be carried from the trough at the rear.

The cut-out stile opposite Bamford Village Green enables a bucket to be carried from the trough at the rear.

One of the four out of five Hathersage Mills that still remain, now converted into accommodation.

Hathersage is a smart, busy village in an attractive location, with Stanage Edge rising steeply to the north and the River Derwent to the south. It is popular with tourists, with its main street lined with shops and eating establishments.

This is all in complete contrast to Hathersage's industrial past, when working conditions were so poor in some of the mills that men seldom lived much over 30 years of age. The dust from the rapidly revolving millstones over which they toiled got into their mouths and lungs until they contracted the dreaded 'grinders' disease'. Four mills still remain, but now have different uses.

Nowadays many visitors come to Hathersage to find out more about its literary connections with Charlotte Brontë, and to walk on the moors as Charlotte did when she stayed here in 1845. During her stay, Charlotte's walks and visits to many of the old houses scattered around the area formed the basis of her famous novel, *Jane Eyre*.

Standing on the hillside above the village is St Michael's Church, which contains a fine collection of 15th-century brasses of the Eyre family, who owned many of the houses visited by Charlotte Brontë on her walks. In the porch is a large 600-year-old stone said to have once marked Little John's (of Robin Hood fame) grave.

The grave was opened in 1784 and a thigh bone 30in in length was exhumed, which would make the occupant over 7ft tall. For many years a great bow and arrow hung in the church. On Stanage Edge is Robin Hood's Cave, which he is supposed to have used as a hideaway, and the Hood Brook flows through the village. Yet it is Nottinghamshire, not Derbyshire, which has reaped the commercial benefits from this legendary figure.

Grindleford is a fairly modern parish, formed as recently as 1987 out of the parishes of Eyam Woodlands, Stoke, Nether Padley and Upper Padley. This ended a lot of confusion, as since the

Little John's grave in St Michael's Churchyard at Hathersage.

14th century the road bridge had been known as Grindleford Bridge. The railway station, although in Nether Padley, was also named Grindleford in the 1890s.

The opening of Totley Tunnel in 1893 and the arrival of the railway benefited the mineral extraction industry at Grindleford Quarry. The railway company used stone, but it most importantly provided an easy means of distribution to more distant places. Over one million tons of gritstone from Grindleford was transported by train for use in the construction of the Howden and Derwent Dams. All this activity brought prosperity to an area where the population was growing rapidly.

The increase in the population after the railway came to Grindleford resulted in the enlargement of the

Queen Victoria and Prince Albert seats in St Michael's Church at Hathersage

37

Totley Tunnel is Britain's second-longest inland railway tunnel, three miles and 950 yards in length.

Commercial Hotel, later renamed the Sir William. The Maynard Arms, built in 1908, near to the railway station, helped to cope with the extra influx of visitors.

On the western side of the bridge over the River Derwent is the Toll Bar Cottage, with the projecting window providing a good view in both directions for the toll keeper to keep a watch out for business. The lovely light and spacious St Helen's Church, consecrated in 1910, five years after the expansion of the Methodist Chapel, is on the opposite side of the road.

Longshaw Estate, with Longshaw Lodge, is situated in excellent walking country on the moors above Grindleford. It was once the Duke of Rutland's shooting estate, but was purchased from the Duke by public subscription in 1927

Grindleford War Memorial, which faces onto the B6001.

Sir William Hotel on the B6001 at Grindleford.

and presented to the National Trust. The estate is very extensive, stretching almost down to Grindleford and including the area around Millstone Edge and Bole Hill, which has a fine collection of abandoned millstones.

The Lodge was built about 1827 to provide a retreat for the Duke of Rutland's shooting guests, among whom included the Duke of Wellington and King George V. After it came into the hands of the National Trust, it was let for a while as a Holiday Fellowship guest house. In 1969 it was converted into private flats.

Grindleford Station Cafe, the home of Grindleford Water.

Longshaw Pastures are well known for the sheepdog trials held there every September. The trials are of interest to both the country lover and the city dweller, and make a wonderful spectacle for visitors and locals alike. The Longshaw Sheepdog Trials claim to be the oldest continuous trials in the country. They started in 1898 and have run to the present day, interrupted only by the two World Wars. Eagerly awaited by enthusiasts, both local and national, they provide sporting entertainment and funds for charity.

Charlotte Brontë

Charlotte Brontë is usually associated with the village of Haworth in Yorkshire, where the family had moved in 1820 when she was four years of age. Her close friend at school was Ellen Nussey, whose brother was vicar of Hathersage. In 1845 Charlotte stayed at the vicarage with Ellen for about three weeks to prepare for the return of the vicar and his wife from honeymoon.

It was from this visit to Hathersage that Charlotte drew the inspiration to write her most famous novel, *Jane Eyre*. Arriving by stage coach, Charlotte was met at the George Inn by the landlord, Mr James Morton, whose surname she is accredited to have used for the fictitious village in her novel.

During her stay, Charlotte took the opportunity to explore, walking on the moors and visiting many of the houses scattered around the area. Several of the places she saw on her walks have almost certainly been included in her book and, although renamed, can be identified from her descriptions.

Thornfield Hall, where Jane meets Rochester, fits the description of North Lees Hall. It was one of seven halls built around Hathersage by Robert Eyre for his seven sons. Visiting the church, Charlotte would have seen the Eyre brasses and have remembered the name.

In August 1847 the novel was published and sold very quickly, although it was not reviewed favourably by all critics. It obtained the royal seal of approval when Queen Victoria read extracts to Prince Albert. Even Charlotte's stern father was impressed and further editions were printed, from which Charlotte earned the substantial sum, in those days, of £500.

Charlotte married Arthur Bell Nicholls in 1854 at Haworth Church, but died the following year. Her name and that of the Brontë family still lives on, however, with thousands of people every year visiting the Brontë Museum in Haworth. The popularity of her book, *Jane Eyre*, and *Wuthering Heights*, which was written by her sister Emily, has never declined.

Nowadays many visitors come to Hathersage to find out more about its literary connections with Charlotte Brontë and to walk on the moors as Charlotte did when she stayed there in 1845.

6
Bamford to Hathersage

The Walk

The River Derwent flows through the eastern side of the Hope Valley, which acts as a magnet to walkers drawn to the area by the variety of the walks available and the magnificent scenery. Many arrive by train from Manchester and Sheffield on the appropriately named Hope Valley Line.

At an early stage of the walk the River Noe, which rises on Kinder Scout, joins the Derwent close to the small hamlet of Shatton. It is a popular starting place for walks on nearby Shatton Moor. As the walk progresses past Kentney Barn it comes to a footpath intersection, where in one direction the river is crossed by stepping stones and the other direction leads off to the right to Offerton Hall.

The Hall is one of seven said to have been built by Robert Eyre for his seven sons, all the buildings built within sight of one another. There is a fine brass impression in Hathersage Church of Ralph Eyre, the sixth son of Robert Eyre, and his wife who lived at the Hall. The present building dates from 1658, but it is thought that a building has stood on the site since the 12th century. It is a classic north Derbyshire manor house, with twin projecting gables and mullioned windows.

The Sheffield train at Bamford Staion, which is part of the popular Hope Valley line.

Mytham Bridge Toll Gate information panel.

After reaching the Grindleford to Hathersage Road, the handsome Leadmill Bridge is crossed, which spans the Derwent in three graceful gritstone arches. It takes its name from the hamlet of Leadmill, which lies on the southern side of the bridge and no doubt got its name from a former lead smelting site. The Plough Inn by the bridge is a popular stopping place.

Between Leadmill Bridge and Hathersage is the Round Building, a purpose-built cutlery factory that has been described as a minor masterpiece of modern architecture. A country shop, museum and café are on-site. The factory is internationally famous for its cutlery, designed by David Mellor. A visit to the museum shows why Mellor is often referred to as the 'Cutlery King'. Mellor is not just famous for cutlery though; in 1966 he designed the national traffic light system, which is still in use to this day. He also designed a square pillar box for the Post Office, but this was not so successful.

Footbridge crossed on the Bamford to Hathersage Walk.

Kentney Barn, passed near the Shatton end of the Bamford to Hathersage Walk.

Leadmill Bridge.

Hathersage today is a large, attractive village with hotels and shops lining the main street. To the north Stanage Edge rises steeply, and to the south flows the River Derwent. In the 19th century the scene was very different; five chimneys belched out black smoke, Hathersage being the centre of the needle, pin and wire-drawing industry. Brass buttons were also manufactured, and in 1847 Samuel Fox designed his Fox Frame lightweight umbrellas. Those industries, along with their smoke, vanished around 1900, although four mills still remain, but now have different uses.

The village has strong literary connections. Charlotte Brontë's best friend at school was Ellen Nussey, whose brother was vicar of Hathersage. In 1845 Charlotte stayed at the vicarage with Ellen for about three weeks to prepare for the return of the vicar and his wife from honeymoon. During her stay Charlotte took the opportunity to explore, walking on the moors and visiting many of the houses scattered around the area. Her famous novel, *Jane Eyre,* was set in Hathersage.

The famous outlaw Robin Hood is said to have been born at Loxley, only eight miles from Hathersage. His lieutenant, Little John, is reputedly buried in Hathersage churchyard, in a grave measuring 11ft from head to footstone.

Nether Hall, passed on the opposite side of the river, on the Bamford to Hathersage Walk.

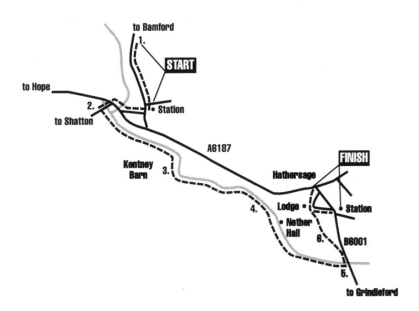

Walk Details

Length: 3.25 miles.

Start/Finish: Bamford (SK208836) – Hathersage Railway Station/Hathersage Village centre.

Starting Walk: The bus stop for both directions is located by the turning circle at the former Mytham Bridge Toll Gate on the A6013, only a short distance from the A618. There are further bus stops and roadside car parking in the centre of the village, from where it is only a short distance down the main road to Mytham Bridge Tollgate. The railway station is on the A6013, near the junction with the A6187. There is a car park for railway users. Limited car parking near Mytham Bridge is available for other users.

Finishing Walk: On reaching Dore Lane, turn right for the railway station and right again at the top of the lane along the B6001. For the bus stops, turn left up Dore Lane and left again

The Plough Inn at Leadmill, which is on the Grindleford side of the bridge.

Stepping stones that present a short cut to Hathersage, unsuitable after heavy rainfall.

at the top, towards the village centre. Bus stops are located near the Little John Public House and on the A6187 in the village centre.

Terrain: Level walking, mostly alongside the River Derwent, with impressive views on either side.

The Route

1. From Bamford walk down the A6013 past Bamford Station; rail users should leave the station by the southern exit. Cross the road and follow the lane down by Mytham Bridge, turning right at the end along the A6187. After passing the High Peak Garden Centre, cross the busy road to enter Shatton Lane.
2. Once you have crossed the bridge over the River Noe, take the footpath on the left, cross a footbridge and climb a short bank. Keep to the path nearest the river, where the path divides.
3. Continue along an obvious path, high up above the river, past Kentney Barn. Later, at a footpath sign, the route descends to follow close to the Derwent, passing stepping stones, which provide a shortcut to Hathersage.
4. Further on, the path is quite narrow in places and requires care. It widens again to pass Nether Hall and go through Goose Nest Wood, before arriving at Leadmill Bridge on the Grindleford to Hathersage road.
5. Cross the bridge and either take the path on the left back to Hathersage, or cross the road and follow the route instructions for the Hathersage to Grindleford walk.
6. For those going to Hathersage/Hathersage Station, follow the clear path through fields to Nether Hall Lodge. For the station, turn right up Dore Lane, at the top of which is the sign for the station. For buses and the village go to the left up the lane, turning left at the top.

7
Hathersage to Grindleford

The Walk

The route follows the Derwent to Coppice Wood, which is part of the National Trust's Longshaw Estate. Here non-rail users continue along the valley to Grindleford, but those bound for the railway station climb up to join a track that passes the ruins of Padley Hall. All that remains of the Hall are part of the foundations and the original gatehouse. Padley Chapel, hidden away on the upper floor of the gatehouse, survives today. It was used as a barn for over 100 years, before being restored in 1933.

On 12 July 1588 Padley Hall was raided and the two Catholic priests, Nicholas Garlick and Robert Ludlam, and several members of the Fitzherbert family were arrested. It was not illegal to be a Catholic, but training abroad to be a priest was against the law. Harbouring a priest was a treasonable offence.

Nicholas Garlick, the son of a Yeoman from Glossop, who had trained to be a priest in France, and Robert Ludlam, the son of a farmer from Radbourne, who had also trained in France, were taken to Derby and hung, drawn and quartered. John Fitzherbert of Padley and his brother both died in prison. A pilgrimage now takes place every year in July when a special service is held in the chapel in memory of the Padley Martyrs.

Most of the walk stays close to the riverbank, unless you are a rail user bound for Grindleford Station.

Burbage Brook near Grindleford
Railway Station Cafe.

Facing Padley Chapel is Brunt's Barn, a volunteer conservation centre opened in 1981 in memory of Harry Brunt for his 'pioneering work for the National Park 1951–80'. A wild flower nursery that propagates an amazing variety of flowers is close by.

Totley Tunnel opened in 1893, but it was a year later before passenger services started. It is Britain's second-longest inland railway tunnel, three miles and 950 yards in length, and took over four years to complete. When it opened it caused considerable excitement in the Sheffield area, opening up, as it did, the rather isolated Hope Valley.

Grindleford was the first stop on the line and the cheapest after the tunnel, and tourists flocked there to see for themselves the glorious land-locked valley. Some liked it so much that they stayed and built their own houses in the area.

Situated in a beautiful setting, with wooded hillsides rising up above the River Derwent, the village of Grindleford occupies a desirable spot. It is a busy place where several roads converge, and before the bridge a ford created an important crossing point over the river for centuries.

Former tollhouse by the river bridge at Grindleford.

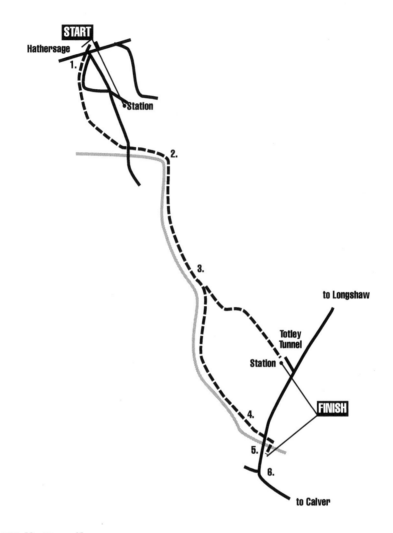

Walk Details

Length: 2 miles.

Start/Finish: Hathersage (SK230815) – Grindleford Railway Station/Grindleford Village centre.

Starting Walk: Hathersage is on the B6001 road from Grindleford. The A6187 Sheffield to Hope Valley road runs through the centre of the village. There is a car park at the station for railway users. Buses stop in the centre of Hathersage, where car parking is also available.

The Peak District and Northern Counties Footpath Society sign by Grindleford Bridge.

Finishing Walk: Turn right down the B6521, cross the bridge and follow the road round to the left to reach Mount Pleasant, where bus stops are on either side of the road. Rail users should follow the instructions in *italics*.

Terrain: An easy stroll down a quiet lane and through fields is followed by a pleasant walk by the River Derwent. Shortly after entering Coppice Wood, rail users climb steeply to reach Padley Chapel – the area around Padley Gorge is stunningly beautiful. Non-rail users continue along the valley floor to Grindleford.

The Route

1. From the village join the B6001 road to Grindleford, shortly turning right down Dore Lane, at the bottom of which follow the path through a series of fields to cross the Grindleford road to a footpath leading to Harper Lees. Rail users should join the B6001 and walk down the road towards Grindleford and, just before reaching Leadmill Bridge, turn left along the private road (also a public footpath) for Harper Lees.

2. Walk down the road until a few yards from Harper Lees House, where you go through a stile on the right. Keep close to the fence on your left, and where it ends keep straight on across a wide field and through a gap in a broken wall to reach the side of the Derwent.

3. Continue with the river close on your right, soon entering Coppice Wood *(*rail users should follow the instructions in italics shown overleaf)*. After leaving the wood remain close to the river until you reach the corner of a long field, where you swing to the left and after about 30 yards go through a gateway into the next field.

4. Keep straight ahead, and as you approach Grindleford the path once again runs close to the river, before reaching the road through the village.

5. Turn right towards the village centre to go to the bus stop. Alternatively, if you wish to continue the walk, refer to the Grindleford

Walking towards Harper Lees.

Harper Lees House, a short distance from the B6001, Hathersage to Grindleford road.

to Calver route section and cross the stile, which is clearly signed on the opposite side of the road, close to Grindleford Bridge.

6. To return to Hathersage by bus, cross the bridge and continue up the road, past bus stops to and from Sheffield, and follow it round to the left to Mount Pleasant, where you will see bus stops (north/south) on either side of the road.

One hundred yards after entering Coppice Wood, rail users should turn left just after crossing a stream. The path follows a hollow way, going to the left at a footpath sign and climbing steeply upwards. At the edge of the wood, turn left over a railway bridge and continue ahead to reach a track. Turn right and follow the track past Padley Chapel and several houses to Grindleford Railway Station.

The walk enters Coppice Wood, where the path divides.

8
Bamford to Grindleford Circular Walk

The Walk

This is a walk to suit all tastes, ranging from attractive river-valley scenery to rugged moorland country that overlooks Hathersage, which has long been a popular centre for walkers and rock climbers. The latter come to test their skills on the gritstone cliff edges of Stanage Edge and Millstone Edge.

The walk follows the River Derwent before climbing up the hillside, passing close to Grindleford Railway Station. It was from Bolehill Quarry, a short distance from the station, that 1.2 million tons of stone was extracted for the construction of Derwent and Howden Dams, which were built between 1901 and 1916. Royal assent for the reservoirs was granted in 1899, and a new railway infrastructure was constructed to assist in transportation.

Close by the quarry are stacks of abandoned cylindrical millstones lying on the ground. Millstones served three main purposes: grinding grain into flour, pulping timber for paper production and as grindstones for the cutlery trade. Stones for pulping timber for the paper industry were exported all over the world between the 1890s and the 1950s, with a few still being exported as late as the 1970s.

Millstones are the symbol of the Peak District National Park, and there is one by the roadside alongside every main road.

The entry to Padley Gorge from the track to Griindleford Station.

The millstones have been abandoned as a result of faulty construction and because demand ceased and nobody wanted to take them away due to their great weight. They can be found in various locations in the Peak District, most particularly near the two main centres of production above Hathersage and Baslow. It is not just walkers who happen to stumble across discarded millstones though; they are the symbol of the Peak District National Park and there is one alongside every main road that enters the park.

The wide green track runs from the former Bolehill Quarry to the A6187.

Hathersage grew rapidly during the Industrial Revolution and became an important centre of manufacture for needles and pins, which were sharpened on grindstones, or millstones, quarried from the edges above the village. It was in the mid 1700s that the rural quiet of the village gradually began to change with the arrival of the wire-drawing industry, although it was nearly 100 years before the industry really took off, following the Great Exhibition when orders started to come in rapidly.

Somewhat cynically, it was said that a wire-drawer was easy to identify because he had several missing fingers. Even more serious were the working conditions for grinders, who seldom lived much over 30 years of age. The dust from the rapidly revolving millstones over which they toiled got into their mouths and lungs until they contracted the dreaded 'grinders' disease'.

Conditions were gradually improved, particularly as a result of a Royal Commission investigating the working environment. The grinders, however, did not always take the precautions advised as they claimed that these slowed productivity. When the industry finally came to an end, Hathersage once again returned to its former peace and quiet.

The village has strong literary connections with Charlotte Brontë, who wrote the famous novel *Jane Eyre* and based it on Hathersage and the surrounding moors. This attracts many visitors, who come to explore the moors and houses around the village described in her book. Tourists are also drawn to the grave in St Michael's churchyard, where Little John, the faithful follower of Robin Hood, is reputedly buried. The grave measures 11ft from head to footstone.

After leaving Hathersage, part of the walk follows an old packhorse route, where ponies laden with panniers full of salt from Cheshire headed across country towards Sheffield and towns further east. Many think that this route was also used by the Romans who forded the Derwent and then ascended Hurst Clough on the way up to Stanage Edge.

A stack of abandoned millstones by the path.

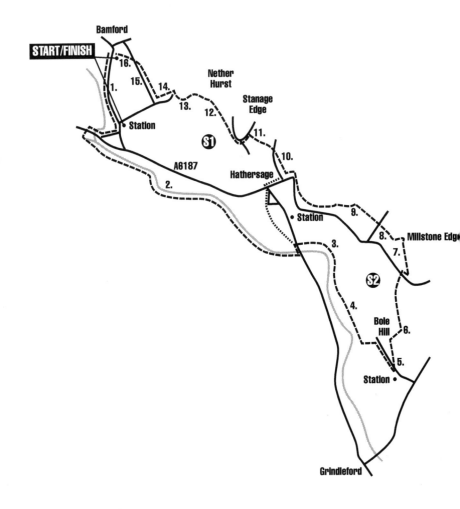

Walk Details

Length: 10.25 miles (Short Walk I – 6.25 miles, Short Walk II – 4.5 miles).

Start/Finish: Bamford Village centre (SK 208836).

Starting/Finishing the Walk: There is no car park, but some roadside parking is available. Bus stops are on either side of the road to the east of the village green/triangle. The railway station is located further down the road near Mytham Bridge Tollgate on the A6013, only a short distance from the A6187. There is a car park for railway users. Limited car parking near Mytham

A wonderful view awaits at 'Surprise View' high above Hathersage on the A6187.

Bridge is available for other users. The bus stop for both directions is located by the turning circle at Mytham Bridge Tollgate.

Terrain: A lovely walk by the River Derwent is followed by a steep climb up to Bole Hill (Ordnance Survey use one word for Bole Hill when referring to Bolehill Wood and Quarry, but not when the name stands alone). Care is needed in following the route for this walk through Bolehill Wood as it is easy to get diverted. Take time to admire the panorama in front of you from Surprise View, before walking across Millstone Edge. The walk from Hathersage to Bamford is comparatively easy, but Hurstclough tends to get waterlogged in wet weather.

The Route

1. Leave Bamford by the A6013, walking down the road past Bamford Railway

Millstone Edge, above Hathersage is a popular spot for climbers.

55

Station and a few yards later turning to the right down a lane by Mytham Bridge, turning right at the end along the A6187. After passing the High Peak Garden Centre, cross the busy road to turn up Shatton Lane.

2. Cross the bridge over the River Noe and take the footpath on the left, cross a footbridge and climb a short bank. Keep to the path nearest the river where it divides. The route continues along an obvious path, high up above the river, past Kentney Barn. Later, at a footpath sign, the path descends to the River Derwent, passing stepping stones, which provide a shortcut to Hathersage. Further on, the path is quite narrow in places and requires care. It widens again to pass Nether Hall and go through Goose Nest Wood, before arriving at Leadmill Bridge on the Grindleford to Hathersage road.

3. Turn left up the B6001 towards Hathersage, cross the bridge and within a few yards go to the right along the private road (also a public footpath) for Harper Lees. Stay on the road until a few yards from Harper Lees House, where you go through a stile on the right. Keep close to the fence on your left, and where it ends carry straight on across a wide field and through a gap in a broken wall to reach the side of the Derwent.

4. Continue with the river close on your right, soon reaching Coppice Wood. Approximately 100 yards after entering the wood, just after crossing a stream, turn left. The path follows a hollow way, going to the left at a footpath sign and climbing steeply upwards. After leaving the wood, turn left over a railway bridge and continue ahead to reach a track. Turn right, passing Padley Chapel and several houses along a track that eventually leads to Grindleford Station.

5. The circular walk that you are following does not go as far as the station, but turns left up a driveway between houses, by a footpath sign for Longshaw via Padley Gorge. At the end of the drive go through a stile and follow the path, which soon bends to the right, before it straightens out and then bends to the right again down a series of steps. Part way down the slope follow the path that forks to the left.

6. Approximately 20 yards after the path starts to swing further to the left, turn sharp left at a fingerpost sign for Surprise View – Bolehill Quarry. Follow a distinct path through the trees and continue ahead at an intersection of paths; soon after, the path swings further to the left to go through a gap in a wall. Then angle to the right and after a few yards go through a stile. Continue ahead for 25 yards, before curving to the right and ascending a short, steep slope. At the top follow the path to the left, with the rock face on your right. A few yards further on, climb up a short, steep stone-lined gulley on your right. At the top, turn right along a path through the bracken that leads to a wide grass track on the left, which you follow all the way to the A6187.

7. On reaching the main road, turn right and walk uphill for 150 yards, before taking the signed path opposite across Millstone Edge. As the path starts to bend sharply to the right, look out for a path on the left. After walking downhill for a short distance with a clearing in front of you, turn sharp left, soon going to the right at an intersection of tracks.

8. Pass some war ruins, and as the path begins to rise go left by a stile into the corner of Whim Wood. Follow the concessionary path through the wood, with the wall close on your right. Leave by a stile in the corner and walk up the road for 50 yards, then go over the stile on the opposite side of the road and down a farm access track.

9. Where the track starts to curve to the right, go to the left across an open field, keeping close to the wall on your left. On reaching the corner, go over a stile and follow a gulley

Pondside Bunkhouse at Nether Hurst.

down, which later becomes an access road to some houses near the A6187. At the bottom, turn right and follow the main road round to the left, going right along Baulk Lane as you drop down to the centre of Hathersage.

10. Follow the lane until after a bend, turn left at a footpath sign and walk diagonally to the right across a field. Go through a stile in the bottom corner of the field and walk for a few yards beside the Hood Brook, before going over a footbridge and heading diagonally to the right up the next field, guided by a series of marker posts to Cliff Wood.

11. Maintain the same direction through the wood, leaving by a stile and keeping close to the fence on the left as you walk towards Birley Farm. Follow a farm track for a few yards behind the farm buildings, before turning left at a fork in the track to go through a gate into a rear farmyard, leaving by a stile to join a lane, where you turn left to walk back past the farmhouse.

12. Turn right at a T-junction of lanes, signed for Bamford Moor, and after 150 yards go to the left at a public bridleway sign. Walk down the field, keeping close to a line of thorn bushes, and maintain the same direction in the next field, keeping close to the fence on your left, to cross a footbridge in the bottom corner. Follow an obvious path up the left-hand side of the field towards Nether Hurst Farm.

13. Go over a stile by a gateway before you reach the farm buildings. Continue forward along an access track, passing Pond Side Bunkhouse, and go through two farm gates to walk along a narrow enclosed track.

14. At the end of the track, continue forward to follow Hurstclough Lane, down a rough cart track. Watch out for a stile on the left, which you go over to descend three fields, keeping close to the right-hand side boundary. Continue along a waymarked path, down a steeply descending incline through woodland, turning right at the bottom along Hurstclough Lane, but only for about 20 yards before going to the left to cross a footbridge and climb up a long series of steps.

15. At the top, turn left to follow the access road round in front of Bamford Filters. Continue in the same direction along Joan Lane, which is very narrow in places.

16. Near the top of a short ascent, go to the left through a squeezer stile and follow a clear path across a field. Continue in the same direction through a housing estate to reach the A6013, a few yards from the starting point of the walk.

Short Walk I

Bamford Walk (6.25 miles)

Route (From Bamford {SK208836} – Mytham Bridge – Hathersage – Baulk Lane – Hurst Clough – Bamford)

1. Follow the Bamford to Grindleford Circular Route instructions from Point 1 to Point 2.

2. Turn left over the bridge, and then left again onto a well-trodden footpath leading up through fields to reach a minor road, which you follow to the left, turning left again at the top of the road to arrive at the A6187 at Hathersage.

3. Walk up the main road and turn left into Baulk Lane to rejoin the Bamford to Grindleford Circular route instructions from Point 10 to Point 16.

Short Walk II

Hathersage Walk (4.5 miles)

Route (From Hathersage {SK230815} – Harper Lees – Bole Hill – Millstone Edge – Hathersage)

1. From the George Hotel in the centre of Hathersage take the B6001 towards Grindleford, passing the train station approach and going under the railway bridge. Before reaching the River Derwent, turn left along a private road (also a public footpath) for Harper Lees.

2. Follow the Bamford to Grindleford route instructions from Point 3 to Point 9.

Refreshment Stops

Plough Inn (Chapter 6/8) is an attractive 17th-century pub, with some outside seating at the front and in a sunken garden at the side, situated on the Grindleford side of Leadmill Bridge. (Tel. 01433 650319)

The path descends a long flight of steps at Hurst Clough.

The views over the Derwent Valley are particularly attractive on the descent to Hathersage.

Bay Tree Coffee Shop (Chapter 6/8) is located within High Peak Garden Centre on the A6187. The walk passes through the garden centre car park. (Tel. 01433 651323)

Little John Hotel (Chapter 6/8) is situated on Station Road at Hathersage. The hotel is named after Robin Hood's second in command, whose grave is allegedly sited in the churchyard at Hathersage. (Tel. 01433 630225)

Sir William Hotel (Chapter 7/8), standing at a height of 1,200ft above sea level, is located approximately 150 yards along the road to Hathersage at Grindleford. (Tel. 01433 630303)

Grindleford Station Café (Chapter 7) is an excellent walker's café, where groups can book early-morning breakfasts at the weekend. There are plenty of tables both inside and out. The café is the home of Grindleford National Spring Water. (Tel. 01433 631011)

Places of Interest in the Locality

Castleton Information Centre is a new state-of-the-art building situated on Buxton Road. It incorporates a small, but very impressive museum, which Castleton Historical Society use to feature a range of exhibitions about village life through the ages. (Tel. 01433 620679)

Castleton Caverns are, without doubt, the most spectacular collection of caverns in the country. For more information contact: Speedwell (Tel. 01433 620512); Blue John (Tel. 01433 620638); Treak (Tel. 01433 620571); Peak (Tel. 01433 620285).

St Michael's Church at Hathersage contains a fine collection of 15th-century brasses of the Eyre family. The famous outlaw Robin Hood is said to have been born at Loxley, only eight miles from Hathersage. His lieutenant, Little John, is reputedly buried in St Michael's Churchyard in a grave measuring 11ft from head to footstone.

David Mellor Cutlery Factory is a masterpiece of modern architecture. The shop beside the factory sells a wide range of cutlery and is open seven days a week. There is also a café, and the factory may be visited during the week. It is situated on the Hathersage side of Leadmill Bridge. (Tel. 01433 650220)

9
Calver, Baslow and the Edges — Colditz

Calver is part of a combined parish of three villages with Curbar and Froggatt, which are both situated higher up the eastern slopes above the Derwent. Calver is the oldest and largest and is the only one of the three mentioned in the *Domesday Book*. The most attractive part of Calver is hidden away behind the main A623 road. Charming stone cottages and smart modern houses exist in comparative harmony close by the ancient village cross. The base of the cross is very old and a standpipe used to be attached to it, from which the villagers could draw water.

The village is composed of three separate settlements laid out in a roughly triangular fashion,

Walking through the ancient village centre at Calver.

with Calver Bridge on the east, Calver Sough in the north and Calver itself filling the remaining area. The sough, which gives the area its name, dates back to the lead mining era. Underground channels were dug, called 'soughs', to free the mines from flooding – the water flowing into a vast subterranean cavern.

It was only after the first bridge had been built across the Derwent and lead mining became popular that the village began to take shape from an isolated community of scattered dwellings. In 1778 a small mill was built close to the new bridge, and this was soon followed by the building of a much larger water-powered cotton mill. The second building was destroyed and replaced by the impressive seven-storey granite building that still remains today. No longer used for industry, it has been converted into luxury apartments. The mill achieved national recognition shortly after World War Two, when it was featured as Colditz, the notorious German POW camp, in a popular television series.

During the Industrial Revolution, the weir on the River Derwent held back water to power the mill. In the years that followed, it was repaired several times, but early this century it was found to be in imminent danger of collapse

The base of the Cross at Calver is very old and a stand pipe used to be attached to it, from where the villagers could draw water.

Calver Methodist Chapel on Main Street.

and requiring urgent repairs. The local residents formed the Calver Mill Weir Liaison Group and obtained a grant to save the structure. Restoration work on the Grade II listed structure began in late 2009 and was completed the following year, at a cost of almost £2 million.

On the Stoney Middleton side of the intersection of the A623 and the B6001 is the former Heginbotham Boot Factory, where steel toe-capped boots were once manufactured. Founded in 1884, it became a major industry in the area and was converted into a limited company in 1920. In the early days the firm ran two small factories in Stoney Middleton, before building a factory in two fields at Calver Sough. The invention and fitting of steel toecaps for miners and for similar trades where the use of the steel cap was beneficial, led to the sale of 40,000 pairs of boots in 1938. As demand reduced, later in the 20th century, boot manufacturing was transferred to Northampton. As a result, the business eventually closed and the premises are now occupied by an outerwear factory shop.

The village of Froggatt sits on the eastern bank of the River Derwent, between Grindleford and Calver, with Froggatt Edge towering above. A feature along the length of the River Derwent, as far as Chatsworth, are the escarpments of gritstone rocks that run along the eastern side of the valley. They

The gate posts on Eatoon Hill are all that is left of the former Baslow Hydro.

St Anne's Church at Baslow is unusual - one clock face has Roman numerals and is dated 1759 and the other has Victoria 1897 instead of numbers.

dominate the skyline from the valley and provide outstanding views for walkers as they stroll along the edges. For those wanting a more energetic pursuit to test their skills, the edges are a good location to practice advanced climbing techniques.

Baslow is a busy little village, delightfully situated in the Derwent Valley, where the limestone country of the White Peak meets the millstone grit of the Dark Peak at the heart of the Peak District. Chatsworth House is only a short walk away to the south, with Baslow Edge rising to the north, from where the short, steep climb is rewarded with fantastic views. The village is full of interest and is well endowed with pubs and places to eat for the many tourists who visit.

Nowadays, the Devonshire Bridge, built shortly after World War One, carries most of the traffic across the river, but it is the Old Bridge,

Dog whip in glass case at Baslow Church.

Walking along the track over Curbar Edge.

Wellington's Monument on Baslow Edge, which celebrates the victory at the Battle of Waterloo in 1815.

close to the church and built in 1603, which attracts most interest from visitors, with its impressive stone arches. It replaced a wooden bridge that all able-bodied men in the village were required to watch on a rota basis to ensure that the weight restrictions were not broken; anyone caught breaking the rules was fined. The tiny watchman's hut still remains, no doubt reduced in size by the heightening of the road. At one time it offered a shelter of sorts to Mary Brady, a local beggar, who often slept rough inside.

The bridge has always played an important role in the history of Baslow, providing an easy route over the moors to Chesterfield and the North Sea ports. Prior to the erection of the first bridge, the ancient trade route crossed a ford near where the bridge now stands. The first turnpike road was built in 1759 from Wardlow to Chesterfield, passing through Little Longstone, Hassop, Baslow and Old Brampton. It is the only bridge across the Derwent never to have been destroyed by floods. To get a better look at the fine workmanship beneath the arches, there is a path you can walk down to the water's edge by the side of the church. This is also an excellent place to watch wildlife and perhaps spot a trout in the river.

As the road network improved, it became easier for wealthy people from Sheffield and other cities to visit the country for health or recreational reasons, and for 50 years Baslow Hydro was the dominating feature in the village. Although falling short of spa status, the Hydropathic Hotel was set in spacious grounds with a croquet lawn, tennis court and bowling green, all surrounded by gardens set out like a miniature park. There were nearly 100 bedrooms, and in the 1890s an annexe was added to provide a further 20 or so bedrooms. Until World War One it was a profitable enterprise, but then trade dwindled and it gradually fell into disrepair, before closing in 1936 and being demolished. All that remain are two stone gateposts.

Baslow Hall stands in landscaped grounds just off the A623 north of the village. It was built in 1907 for Revd Jeremiah Stockdale, vicar of Baslow for 48 years, and it became the home of electrical pioneer Sebastian de Ferranti in 1913. Ferranti was a DIY enthusiast with a passion for electricity. He experimented with central heating and other electrical appliances, in addition to fitting double glazing. Sadly, his efforts at battery poultry farming had disastrous consequences for the chickens, who were electrocuted. It is now a hotel and restaurant.

Rock formations along Curbar Edge.

Colditz

Calver Mill first achieved national recognition sometime after the Second World War when it featured as *Colditz*, the notorious German POW camp, in a popular television series based on Pat Reid's account of the prisoners-of-war life at Colditz Castle. When viewers saw prisoners escaping across the roof, it was Calver Mill they were seeing and not the roof and walls of Schloss Colditz.

During the series the swastika flew high above the mill, but no one was fooled. This was not the case during the war itself, when lights were lit on the moors nearby, fooling the German bomber pilots into thinking that Sheffield lay below and releasing their loads harmlessly onto the moors.

A cotton mill and a small weir were built in 1778 by John Pares and John Gardom, hosiers and yarn merchants. Seven years later it had been replaced by a three-storey building. Disaster struck in 1799, when severe floods swept away Calver Bridge and took part of the mill with it. Further misfortune followed three years later when the mill was burnt down. A new larger mill, six storeys in height was constructed, which began production in 1804. Just over 25 years later it employed 200 workers.

The late 1800s saw several changes of ownership and cotton spinning at the mill came to an end in 1923. The mill was little used prior to the Second World War, when it was used as a storage depot. After the war the mill was a depressing site of neglect and decay. Rehabilitation was at hand, after Gordon Sissons had taken a look at the mill, while out on a bicycle ride from his home in Grindleford. Shortly afterwards, it was purchased by Sissons firm, W. & G. Sissons, a long-established Sheffield firm of stainless steel manufacturers.

Soon after the death of Gordon Sissons the factory closed, with some of the work being transferred to Sheffield. In recent years the mill has been converted into high class accommodation. The national fame it achieved through the television series as *Colditz* long forgotten.

10
Grindleford to Calver

The Walk

The starting point of this attractive valley walk from Grindleford village is marked by an ornate cast iron sign designed for the Peak and Northern Footpath Preservation Society. Apart from indicating the route to follow, it also informs you that you are 427ft above sea level.

The path soon enters Horse Hay Coppice, which is owned by the National Trust, as is Froggatt Wood, which quickly follows with no noticeable change in the terrain. The sides of the valley are littered with huge boulders and wooded with silver birch, oak and ash, and the land is covered with a carpet of wild flowers during the spring and summer. The higher ground beneath Froggatt Edge is dominated by bracken and bilberry, which provides a wonderful sight, particularly in the autumn, when the bracken turns a lovely golden colour set against the rocks towering above.

The Duke of Rutland originally owned the village of Froggatt, and farmers and stonemasons used to occupy the attractive stone cottages, but they are now mostly the homes of commuters and retirees. Above the village, the edges are a popular area for rock climbers and walkers. Froggatt Bridge, a substantial stone-built construction, provides excellent views up and down the river. It was built in the 17th century and is unusual in having a large central arch on the village side and a smaller arch on the far side. This was probably because the bridge was extended following the widening of the river when the Derwent was dammed at Calver.

The National Trust sign at the entrance to Horse Hay Coppice.

A beautiful woodland Walk
between Grindleford and Froggatt.

After crossing New Bridge, the attractive, eye-catching 18th-century Shuttle House looks out across the river. It originally housed the sluice machinery to control the speed of the water from the river to power Calver Mill. A short distance further along the river, a huge pool has been created by a substantially sized weir. A Grade II listed structure, the reconstruction of the weir was completed in 2010. This involved not only repairing the weir itself, but also putting in a fish pass, creating new paths and improving access for disabled people.

As you walk down Duke's Drive, which was used by the Duke of Rutland

The River Derwent near Calver.

Cottage near Froggatt Bridge, which is unusual in having a large central arch on the village side and a smaller arch on the other.

Shuttle House, which originally held the sluices to control the water speed.

on his journey from Haddon to his shooting lodge at Longshaw, through the trees on your right you will catch glimpses of the mill that achieved national recognition shortly after World War Two. It was featured as Colditz, the notorious German POW camp, in a popular television series. During the series, the swastika flew high above Calver Mill.

It was only after the first bridge had been built across the Derwent and lead mining became popular that Calver began to take shape from an isolated community of scattered dwellings. It now forms a combined parish of three villages with Curbar and Froggatt, but Calver is the oldest and largest.

The Bridge Inn at Calver from where the villages two bridges (the 'old' and the 'new') can be viewed.

Walk Details

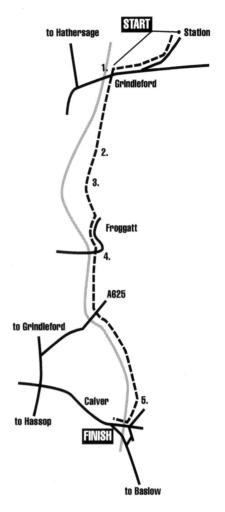

Length: 3 miles.

Start/Finish: Grindleford Village centre
(SK244778) – Grindleford Station/Calver
Bridge.

Starting Walk Roadside car parking is
available near the bridge and in the centre of
the village. Rail users from Grindleford
Station and car park should walk towards the
B6521 and turn to the right shortly before
reaching the road, along a path that soon
leads you down to the B6521, where you
turn right again. After passing the church,
look out for a stile on the left – this is where
you start the walk to Calver Bridge. Bus and
car users from the village centre should
follow Point 1.

Finishing Walk: Bus stops are located on
the A623, close to the Bridge Inn. To continue
the walk, go to the Calver to Baslow route
section.

Terrain: Rail users have a steady descent
from Grindleford Station to within a few
yards of the bridge over the River Derwent at
Grindleford. Non-rail users start from the
centre of the village. The walk soon goes
through woodland, before joining Spooner
Lane and arriving in the pretty village of
Froggatt. The remainder of the route follows
a clear path through woodland close to the River Derwent, then down Duke's Drive to Calver.

The Route
1. From the centre of Grindleford, non-rail users should head east along the B6521, cross the
   bridge over the Derwent and turn right at an ornate footpath sign. Walk diagonally across a
   field, away from the river, to ascend a slope to enter Horse Hay Coppice.
2. Follow the main path through the wood, leaving by a squeezer stile. Cross the middle of a
   field, and in the next field continue ahead, staying close to the wall. Just before reaching the
   corner of the field, go through a stile on your right.
3. The path angles down the next field, before straightening out and going through a stile by
   a metal gate to enter Spooner Lane, which you follow to the small village of Froggatt.

Calver Gallery, formerly a post office and shop.

Calver Mlil was featured as 'Colditz,' the notorious German POW camp, in a popular television series is seen in the background.

4. At a T-junction, go right down Hollowgate to Froggatt Bridge. Do not cross the bridge, but carry straight on along Froggatt Lane for 75 yards, before crossing a stile on the right.
5. Follow the path by the Derwent, crossing a road after about half a mile, until you reach Duke's Drive on the outskirts of Calver. Walk down the road for 350 yards and turn right opposite the Bridge Inn to reach Calver Bridge.

Path approaching Duke's Drive, which was used by the Duke of Rutland on his journey from Haddon to his shooting lodge.

11
Calver to Baslow

The Walk

Calver is soon left behind on this popular walk to Baslow, and after crossing two fields St Mary's Wood is entered. On the opposite side of the River Derwent is Cliff College, set back a short distance from the A623. It is a Christian theological college and was founded by Henry Grattan Guinness in 1883. Here Biblical Theology is taught at undergraduate level, and a number of mission courses for postgraduates are also undertaken. Above the College, Baslow Edge rises steeply, providing magnificent views for those prepared to ascend the steep paths from Calver or Baslow. The wild, heather-clad moorland, which was once home to Bronze Age farmers, is now the habitat of merlin and grouse, with highland cattle patrolling the moors, seemingly enjoying the view.

After a relaxing riverside walk, the path moves away from the Derwent to reach Bubnell Lane. A short distance down the lane, Bubnell Hall, thought to be the oldest building in the parish, is passed. It is an attractive building that at one time was a school. Looking across the weir, the houses at Bridge End can be seen with their attractive

Calver Mill is now used for accommodation.

Walkers approaching Bubnell on the walk from Calver.

River Derwent viewed from Calver Bridge.

river frontages. Behind them is Baslow Hall, the former home of Sebastian de Ferranti, who lived at the hall in the early 20th century.

Bubnell is on the west bank of the River Derwent, north of the bridge, and most of the village of Baslow is on the eastern side of the river. Bridge End is the original settlement, clustered around the church and the ancient bridge and ford across the River Derwent. The Old Bridge, close to the church and built in 1603, attracts much interest from visitors with its impressive stone arches; it is the oldest bridge across the Derwent never to have been destroyed by floods.

It replaced a wooden bridge that all able-bodied men in the village were required to watch on a rota basis to ensure that the weight restrictions were not broken; anyone caught breaking the rules was fined. The tiny watchman's hut still remains, no doubt reduced in size by the heightening of the road.

St Anne's is both a beautiful and unusual church – one clock tower has Roman numerals and is dated 1759, while the other has 'Victoria 1897' on its face to mark Queen Victoria's Golden

Visitors relaxing by the river at Baslow at the bottom of the path by the church.

Watchman's Hut on the Old Bridge at Baslow, no doubt reduced in size by the heightening of the road.

St Anne's Church at Baslow.

Jubilee. Inside the church, by the door in a glass case, is a dog whip, which in the 17th and 18th centuries was used by the official 'dog whipper' to keep stray dogs in order during the service. The whip has a leash 3ft long, which is still in excellent condition and is bound around the handle with leather. Some historians also claim that it was used to maintain order among worshippers and to wake up those who snored during the service!

A cross lies in the churchyard, which was moved from Bubnell by Doctor Wrench, who erected the Wellington Monument on Baslow Edge. The cross may historically have been known as the 'Butter Cross'. Doctor Wrench is buried in the churchyard.

The most popular part of the village with visitors is Nether End with its hotels and little shops set around Goose Green, where people can sit in comfort and relax. From here the parklands of Chatsworth are approached over a 17th-century Packhorse Bridge and past a row of pretty thatched cottages. It is one of the best short walks in the county, opening up as it does the delights of a visit to Chatsworth House and a stroll in the park and gardens.

The Old Bridge at Baslow viewed from the park by the church.

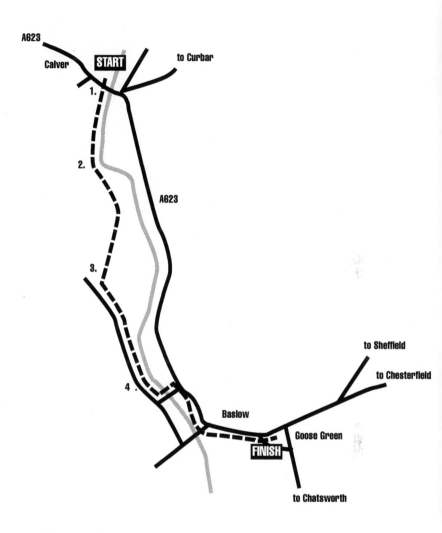

Walk Details

Length: 2 miles.

Start/Finish: Calver Bridge (SK245746) – Goose Green, Baslow.

Starting Walk: Off the A623 Baslow to Stoney Middleton Road, Calver Bridge is at the rear of the Bridge Inn. Buses stop on the A623, close to the Bridge Inn. Car parking is available in the village.

The 17th century Packhorse Bridge at Baslow.

Finishing Walk: Buses stop close to the car park at Goose Green, off the A619. To continue the walk, go to the Baslow to Chatsworth House route section.

Terrain: A lovely, easy valley walk, then a stroll down Bubnell Lane, with its interesting houses on one side of the road and the river on the other, to the fascinating village of Baslow.

The Route

1. On the western side of Calver Bridge, take the path by the river, close to the grassed area, which leads you under the subway in front of a row of houses.
2. After leaving the houses behind, continue by the river through two fields to enter a wood as the river bends to the left. The path continues close to the river, before swinging away to the right and eventually leaving the wood.
3. Continue with the wall on your left, before angling slightly to the right to a stile. Then cross a field diagonally to a stile onto a lane.
4. Turn left down Bubnell Lane. After passing the weir, turn left across the Old Bridge at Baslow. Go to the right in front of the church and continue straight on at a major road junction to Goose Green, where there is a large car park, shop, café and several pubs and restaurants.

12
Grindleford to Baslow Circular Walk

The Walk

An exhilarating walk with superb views that takes you along the Derwent Valley before climbing up to the gritstone edges of Baslow, Curbar and Froggatt. The climb up to Baslow Edge is the most strenuous part of the route, and here it is worth taking a short diversion for a closer look at Wellington's Monument, which celebrates the victory at the Battle of Waterloo in 1815. The

monument was built by Lieutenant Colonel E.M. Wrench, who took over a medical practice in Baslow in 1862. He was a surgeon who had served in the army in both Crimea and India. He was a great patriot, and in 1866 he had the 10ft-high cross on Baslow Edge constructed so that it could be seen over a wide area.

Standing in solitary confinement on Baslow Edge is a massive boulder, known as the Eagle Stone. According to legend, it took its name from the god Aigle, who it appeared had a habit of throwing

The ornate footpath sign at the starting point for the Grindleford to Baslow Circular Walk.

Beautiful scenery on climb up to Baslow Edge.

The Eagle Stone on Baslow Edge is a prominent landmark, which the young men of the village were expected to climb before they could marry.

boulders around. In the past, no local lad was considered fit to marry until he had shown his fitness and agility by climbing to the top of the stone.

Baslow Edge is separated from Curbar Edge by Curbar Gap, where a Roman road once passed through. It later became an important packhorse route to Chesterfield, and in 1759 the road was turnpiked. There is an old guide stoop, which dates back to those days, next to the busy pay-and-display car park. Alongside the footpath to Baslow, below Curbar Gap, are the Cundy Graves. The family of five all died of the Great Plague, just over 30 years prior to the epic struggle of the people of Eyam. In a period of just over 12 months from September 1665, 260 people out of a population of about 800 died from the Plague.

There are more Curbar plague graves to be found below the Wesleyan Reform Chapel, lower down the village. Until the early 1920s Curbar was part of the Duke of Rutland's Estate. It is now made up of an interesting collection of old privately owned cottages that climb up the hillside

Baslow Edge is strewn with rocks of many different sizes.

close to the old Roman road, and smart modern properties built in recent years.

About two miles after leaving Curbar Gap behind, where the track begins to bend in a northerly direction, is a small stone circle, partly hidden in the heather. According to archaeological research, a sizeable number of Bronze Age people once lived in the vicinity of the stone circle. Opinion is divided as to whether this was a permanent or a seasonal settlement.

The 1977 Jubilee Gardens, by the bridge at Grindleford, is a pleasant place to sit and relax. Across the road, more strenuous activity takes place on Bridgefields Sports Ground. The large, well-equipped Bishop Pavilion, apart from providing sporting facilities, acts as the centre of community life in the village. Further up the village street, on the site of the former Red Lion pub, is a group of cottages that carries the pub's name. Opposite is the Derwent Gallery, selling pictures of the Peak District.

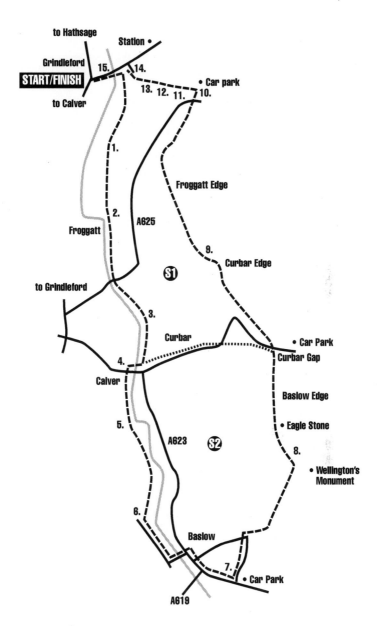

Walk Details

Length: 9.5 miles (Short Walk I – 6.5 miles, Short Walk II – 5 miles).

Start/Finish: Grindleford Village centre (SK244778).

Starting/Finishing Walk: Grindleford is situated at a road junction between the B6001 to Hathersage and the B6521 to Longshaw. There is no public car park, but roadside parking is available. Buses travelling north to south stop at Mount Pleasant, from where you follow the road round to the bridge. Grindleford Railway Station and car park are to be found about one mile from the village centre, off the B6521 in the Longshaw direction. To join the walk from the railway station, take the path leading off the station approach road and follow it down to the B6521, where you turn right and walk down to the footpath by Grindleford Bridge.

Terrain: A woodland walk by the side of the River Derwent is followed by a long, steep ascent to Baslow Edge, where the views are stunning, as they are from Curbar and Froggatt Edge a little further along the route. Take care when leaving the path to have an even better look at the views and keep well clear of the cliff edges. The final part of the walk descends quite steeply through woodland back to Grindleford.

The Route

1. From the centre of Grindleford head east along the B6521, cross the bridge over the Derwent and turn right at an ornate footpath sign. Walk diagonally across a field away from the river to ascend a slope to enter Horse Coppice Wood. Follow the main path through the wood, leaving by a squeezer stile, cross the middle of a field and in the next field continue ahead, staying close to the wall. Just before reaching the corner of the field, go through a stile on your right.

2. The path angles down the next field, before straightening out and going through a metal gate to enter Spooner Lane, which you follow to the small village of Froggatt. At a T-junction, go right down Hollowgate to Froggatt Bridge. Do not cross the bridge, but carry straight on along Froggatt Lane for 75 yards, before crossing a stile on the right.

3. Follow the path by the Derwent, crossing a road after about half a mile, until you reach Duke's Drive on the outskirts of Calver. Walk down the road for 350 yards and turn right opposite the Bridge Inn to reach Calver Bridge.

4. Cross the bridge to the western side and take the path by the river, close to the grassed area, which leads you under the subway to pass in front of a row of houses.

Climbing up to the edge of the gritstone escarpment for a better view of the Derwent Valley.

The view from Froggatt Edge is stunning.

5. After leaving the houses behind, continue by the river through two fields to enter a wood as the river bends to the left. The path continues close to the river, before swinging away to the right and eventually departing the wood. Continue with the wall on your left, before angling slightly to the right to a stile, then diagonally across a field to a stile onto a lane.

6. Turn left down Bubnell Lane. After passing the weir, turn left across the Old Bridge at Baslow. Go to the right in front of the church and continue straight on at a major road junction to Goose Green. Here there is a large car park, shop, café and several pubs and restaurants.

7. Cross the busy A619 at Goose Green by the pedestrian lights and walk to the right of a restaurant up Eaton Hill. At a T-junction, turn right up Bar Road, which soon turns into a rough track. Follow the track as it bends first to the right and then left past Ladywell Farm. At the top of the climb, you may wish to take a short detour to the right to visit Wellington's Monument, before turning left along a wide track across the open moor.

8. Soon you pass a massive boulder known as the Eagle Stone as you follow the track across the moor. At the end of the moor, with Curbar Gap in sight, you reach two stiles divided by a metal gate; take the stile on the left.

9. Cross the road and ascend the path opposite onto Curbar Edge and follow the well-defined unbroken path along Curbar Edge and Froggatt Edge. After about two miles the path leads you to a stile by a gate to enter an area of woodland, where you follow the clear path to the A625.

10. Turn right and walk up the road for 25 yards, before going through a stile on the opposite side of the road. The path descends fairly steeply for a few yards to a small stream, which you cross and walk up the other side, where you will see the Haywood car park in front of you.

11. Do not enter the car park, but go to the left where the path divides and left again after 25 yards, down a short slope to go through a stile at the bottom.
12. Follow the path downhill through woodland for 150 yards and, just as the path ahead begins to rise, take the left-hand fork and continue downhill. Ignore all the paths to the right and left and continue to descend, soon arriving at a National Trust sign indicating that you have been passing through Longshaw Estate – Haywood.
13. Continue down a wide, rough woodland access road for a short distance to reach the end of the wood.
14. Turn right and walk along an access road for several houses, which bends to the left and straightens out to meet the B6521 by St Helen's Church at Grindleford.
15. Go to the left down the road (railway station users go in the opposite direction), past the former toll house, opposite to which is the footpath that you used at the start of the walk. Cross the bridge over the River Derwent to reach the centre of the village, passing local bus stops. For the bus stops (north/south), follow the road round to the left to Mount Pleasant.

Short Walk I

Grindleford Walk (6.5 miles)
Route (From Grindleford {SK244778} – Froggatt – Calver – Baslow – The Edges – Haywood – Grindleford)

1. Follow the Grindleford to Baslow circular route instructions from Point 1 to Point 3 to the end of Duke's Drive.
2. Turn sharp left with the side of All Saints Church facing you across the road, walk up Curbar Lane, signed for Curbar Village.
3. Continue up the long hill, carrying straight on when the road bends to the left, through a stile and follow a steep, winding path to meet the road again as it bends back to the right near Curbar Gap.
4. Walk along the verge by the road for a short distance, before crossing the road to rejoin the Grindleford to Baslow circular route instructions from Point 9 to Point 15.

Short Walk II

Baslow Walk (5 miles)
Route (From Baslow {SK259721} – Bar Road – Eagle Stone – Curbar Gap – Curbar – Calver – Baslow)

1. Follow the Grindleford to Baslow circular route instructions from Point 7 to Point 8.
2. On reaching Curbar Gap, turn left and walk down the grass verge by the road for a short distance, before going over a stile on the left.
3. Continue down the hill to follow a steep and winding path, which rejoins the road some distance below Curbar Gap.
4. Follow the road straight down to All Saints Church, which is on your left at the bottom, with Duke's Drive on your right.
5. From this point you turn right towards Calver Bridge and follow the Grindleford to Baslow circular route instructions from Point 4 to Point 6.

Baslow Village Spar Shop with an old delivery bicycle at the forefont.

Refreshment Stops

Bridge Inn (Chapter 10/12) at Calver is a small, friendly pub with two bars and a large garden running down to the River Derwent, from where the village's two bridges can be viewed. (Tel. 01433 630415)

Derbyshire Craft Centre (Chapter 10/12), which is situated close to the new bridge at Calver, has on display a large selection of local and national crafts, plus a wide range of gifts, books and other items. There is also a popular café. (Tel. 01433 631231)

Café on the Green (Chapter 11/12) is pleasantly furnished and looks out over Goose Green at Baslow. It was formerly known as the Goose Green Café. (Tel. 01246 583000)

Wheatsheaf Hotel (Chapter 11/12), Nether End, Baslow is situated close to the Chesterfield Road and Goose Green. It is a large, spacious pub. (Tel. 01246 582240)

Places of Interest in the Locality

Padley Chapel is an early 14th-century gatehouse and chapel; it is all that remains of Padley Manor House, the home of two Roman Catholic families who were persecuted for their beliefs. Two priests from here were executed.

Longshaw Visitor Centre is situated in the outbuildings of Longshaw House, in wonderful walking country with magnificent views. It is a popular place to stop and perhaps purchase a gift from the National Trust shop. (Tel. 01433 631708)

Eyam is a fascinating place to explore. It is most remembered for its tragic history, when so many people died as a result of the Great Plague. Eyam Museum and plaques around the village tell the story. The Craft Centre and Eyam Hall are also popular places to visit.

Hassop Railway Station on the Monsal Trail was built much nearer to Bakewell than to Hassop in order to serve the Duke of Devonshire. It is very ornate, no doubt to please the Duke. Now the railway is no more; it has been converted into a spacious bookshop. (Tel. 01629 813444)

13
The Villages and Communities around Chatsworth – Joseph Paxton

Chatsworth, 'The Palace of the Peak', was named Britain's Best Stately Home in *Period Living and Traditional Homes* magazine's Best of British Awards 2004–05. Over 200,000 votes were cast when readers of the market-leading magazine were asked to nominate the aspects of traditional British life that they love best.

The first house at Chatsworth was built by Bess of Hardwick and her second husband, Sir William Cavendish. Building began in 1552 and the work was completed by his widow after Sir William died in 1557.

Today, Chatsworth is one of the Treasure Houses of England, with fine furniture, sculpture, tapestry, paintings and other works of art. Set in beautiful surroundings in the heart of the Peak District National Park, it attracts admiring visitors from all over the world.

Laid out by 'Capability' Brown in the 1760s, the 1,000-acre park is mostly open to the public free of charge throughout the year. The grass is grazed by sheep, cattle and a large herd of deer, which can usually be seen as you walk through the park. The road that winds its way through the parkland provides a magnificent view of Chatsworth House.

The estate villages of Beeley, Edensor and Pilsley are, without doubt, three of the most attractive villages in the Peak National Park. They tend to share facilities: Pilsley has the school and a pub, Edensor a church and institute, and Beeley a church and a pub. Both pubs are called the Devonshire Arms, which can cause confusion at times. There are tea shops in all the villages, the one at Pilsley being part of the highly successful farm shop complex.

The small estate village of Edensor, pronounced 'Ensor', is set in one of the most beautiful locations in the country, in parkland owned by the Devonshire family, whose stately home at Chatsworth House is only five minutes walk away. Mentioned in the *Domesday Book*, the village has been resited since then. Originally, when the houses were set out in a straggling line down to the Derwent, it lay between the river and the road through the park.

This did not appeal to the fourth Duke of Devonshire, who, having spent considerable money and effort improving the House, redesigning the gardens and building a grand new bridge over the

river, decided to take down those houses visible from the House. The tenants were rehoused in the nearby estate villages of Pilsley and Beeley. The sixth Duke completed the dismantling of the old village and built the present one.

Joseph Paxton, who remodelled and landscaped the gardens at Chatsworth, chose the site for the new village, but it

Pig Lane, Beeley, which at one time was the main road through the

Beeley Brook babbles contentedly along Brookside at Beeley.

was John Robertson, a relatively unknown architect from Derby, who provided the designs. At that time, aspiring young architects such as Robertson would prepare a book of house plans as part of their training.

It is thought that Robertson approached the Duke to show him the plans when he was busy with other matters, and that after quickly looking through them the Duke could not make up his mind and chose all the different styles in the book. The designs, ranging from Norman to Jacobean, Swiss-style to Italian villas, are all here at Edensor. A few of the old houses remained virtually untouched, including parts of the old vicarage, two cottages overlooking the green and the old farmhouse, which now houses the village shop and tea rooms.

At the top of the churchyard is the grave of Kathleen Kennedy, the sister of the late President of the USA. She was the wife of the late Duke's elder brother and heir to the dukedom. The Duke's brother was tragically killed in Belgium during World War Two, and only four years later his wife was killed in an air crash.

In June 1963 John F. Kennedy, the thrn President of the United States, visited the grave – five months before being assassinated – on his way by helicopter to a meeting with the Prime Minister. This event is recalled by the Duchess of Devonshire in her book, *The House: a Portrait of Chatsworth*, when she describes the reaction of one resident of the village, 'The wind from that machine blew my chickens away and I haven't seen them since.'

Looking down School Lane at Beeley towards the Devonshire Arms.

The path from opposite the gates at Edensor to Chatsworth House.

Beeley is a pretty, unspoilt village sheltered by Beeley Moor, with wonderful views in all directions. It had acquired its present shape and size by 1800. With the exception of a small group of properties built in recent years on the Chesterfield Road, it has remained remarkably unchanged for over 200 years. The same does not apply to the use of the buildings: the school, schoolhouse, post office and reading room are all now private houses. Duke's Barn, built in 1791 to house the estate carts used to carry coal from Rowsley Station, is now a residential study centre.

What makes the village so beautiful is that almost all the farm and domestic buildings are built from the same honey-coloured sandstone, quarried locally, close to Fallinge Edge. The local stone quarries once gave employment to a large number of men. The two quarries at Bruntwood produced stone not only of good appearance, but also of such hard-wearing quality that it was used in many of the principle buildings in Manchester.

There are two Pilsleys in Derbyshire: the former mining village near to Clay Cross in North East Derbyshire, and the Chatsworth Estate Village described in this section. It is an attractive, unspoilt village lying about one mile east of Chatsworth House, with magnificent views over the Derwent Valley.

The limestone cottages are enriched by gardens full of colour, many of the occupiers having learned the craft of gardening in the gardens at Chatsworth House. Some describe it as a sleepy little village, but fail to take into account that the popular Chatsworth Farm Shop is located in Pilsley. It has been so successful that further expansion of the Farm Shop has taken place, including an enlargement of the restaurant facilities.

In 1839 Paxton built the village school and some of the other houses in the village, but not the group near to the Devonshire Arms, which were built more than a century earlier. Many of the houses round the green were constructed during the period when the sixth Duke of Devonshire was knocking down and rebuilding Edensor out of sight of Chatsworth House.

Edensor originally lay between the river and the road through the Park, before being resited.

Edensor Shop and Café, a popular spot with walkers.

Joseph Paxton

Joseph Paxton was born on 3 August 1803, in Milton Bryan, Bedfordshire, very close to the Woburn Estate of the Duke of Bedford. He was the seventh son of a yeoman farmer. He is best known as the designer of the Crystal Palace, which was built to house the Great Exhibition, held at Hyde Park in 1851, and later moved to Sydenham Hill. However, this remarkable man had many other achievements besides becoming the foremost horticulturist of his time. He wrote extensively, took a leading part in founding a national newspaper, designed public parks, promoted railway expansion and was the architect of large number of buildings, including railway stations. Also he served as MP for Coventry for 11 years.

In his teens he worked at Battlesden Park as a garden boy and had a number of other gardening jobs. He then began working at Chiswick Gardens, which was leased by the Horticultural Society from the Duke of Devonshire. The Duke was so impressed by his ability that in 1826, he appointed him as head gardener at Chatsworth. On his first day he arrived at Chatsworth at 4.30am, having travelled from London to Chesterfield by the Comet Coach. As no one was available to greet him, he explored the grounds, made

The gravestone of Kathleen Kennedy, Sister of the former President of the USA in Edensor Churchyard.

Devonshire Arms at Pilsley decorated for the Well Dressings.

plans for the future and later set the men to work, before having breakfast with Mrs Gregory, the housekeeper, and her niece, with whom he fell in love and eventually married. All this before nine o'clock in the morning!

In 1829 he was made head forester and began the process of putting the estate woodlands back into shape after a long period of neglect. He planted the pinetum, a comprehensive collection of pines, many of them new to this country. Large trees were carefully moved from locations outside Chatsworth and planted in the grounds. In 1835 he started work on an arboretum and seven years later he built rockworks on the hillside, with waterfalls and cascades. He oversaw the replacement of the estate village of Edensor and constructed the Emperor Fountain. This was built in 1844 to impress Czar Nicholas of Russia. Unfortunately, the Czar was detained elsewhere and failed to visit Chatsworth. The fountain's single gravity fed high spout, rises to 290ft and is the tallest in Britain. Paxton also built a conservatory – known as the Great Conservatory – and a lily house, specially designed for a giant lily with a design based on the leaves of the plant.

Paxton used the designs he had implemented at Chatsworth as a basis for the plans he put forward for his successful design of the Crystal Palace in Hyde Park, London. The building went on to house the 'Great Exhibition of the Works of All Nations' in 1851. Two hundred and forty five designs were submitted for the building, but all were considered either too expensive or impossible. At the very last minute Paxton was asked to produce a design, which he did on a sheet of blotting paper. The plans gained public support after publication in the Illustrated London News and were accepted The building itself was erected in just six months, with 293,655 panes of glass, 330 huge iron columns and 24 miles of gutters.

Failing health forced Paxton to retire from Parliament in the spring of 1865 and on the 8 June of that year he died. He is buried in the churchyard of St Peter's Church at Edensor, in a grave of much grander scale than that of his master, the sixth Duke.

14
Baslow to Chatsworth House

The Walk

On leaving Goose Green, the walk crosses a 17th-century packhorse bridge and passes a row of pretty thatched cottages, unusual for the Peak District where thatching is quite rare. A short distance away on the right is The Cavendish Arms, one of the Peak District's best-known hotels, which is also famous for the 10 miles of trout fishing it offers visitors.

Chatsworth Park is entered through the skilfully designed Cannon Kissing Gate. The gate, opened in March 1999, was the idea of Mrs Jill Cannon to provide access to the park for wheelchair users. The gate was made and donated by Mathers Engineering and allows wheelchair access to the park without leaving an opening through which grazing stock might escape.

Shop at Goose Green, Baslow, which is a magnate for visitors in the summer.

Thatched cottages on the route to Chatsworth Park.

The Cannon Kissing Gate designed for wheelchairs and to keep animals from straying.

Further along the path, the White Lodge and plant nursery are passed, as well as the attractive Chatsworth Cricket Ground. The Hunting Tower can be seen in the distance, standing on an escarpment 400ft above Chatsworth House, on the edge of Stand Wood. Completed *c.*1582 for Bess of Hardwick, ancestress of the Dukes of Devonshire, the Tower was designed by the famous Elizabethan architect Robert Smythson. It is now available as a holiday let for groups.

Stand Wood is an historic stretch of woodland, situated to the north of the house. It is open all year to visitors, and during the visitor season tractor tours are available. The woodland provides an impressive backdrop to Chatsworth House and contains a rich diversity of trees and wildlife. The views across the park are magnificent, particularly so from the Hunting Tower, one of the few survivors from the days of Bess of Hardwick.

Estate workers tidying up Chatsworth Park.

White Lodge is passed on the route through the park.

Every year the park is host to the Chatsworth International Horse Trials, which are among the most prestigious in the country and attract the world's best riders. Horse trials first took place at Chatsworth as far back as the 1950s; in the 1980s Chatsworth hosted an international three-day event, and the idea of running horse trials was reinstated in 1999.

The three-part sport of horse trials – or eventing – is the most demanding and intriguing of all equestrian sport, as it places the emphasis on trust and versatility in the partnership between rider and horse, who have to show obedience and grace in the dressage phase, courage and athleticism in cross country, and accuracy in showjumping.

The Country Fair, held annually in the park, is one of England's most spectacular annual outdoor events. It attracts large crowds from all over the country. Massed pipe and military bands, demonstrations and parades, hot-air balloons, parachuting and over 300 varied trade stands and rural crafts make this a memorable event with something for everyone. Many of England's traditional country sports and pastimes are on show, including armed service displays, horse shoeing, ferret racing, archery and sheepdog trials.

The Bower near the main drive to the house has taken the name Queen Mary's Bower following Mary, Queen of Scots, being held a prisoner at Chatsworth five times between 1570 and 1581. Here, it is thought, she was allowed to exercise in a secure environment.

The deer in Chatsworth Park are a popular attraction.

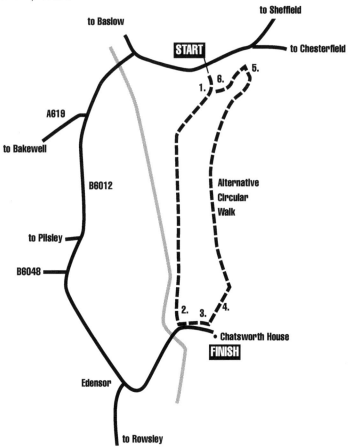

Walk Details

Length: 1.25 miles, or approximately 3 miles if the alternative return route is used.

Start/Finish: Goose Green, Baslow (SK259721) – Chatsworth House {Different return route to Baslow also detailed.}

Starting Walk: Goose Green is on the left as you enter Baslow on the A623 from Chesterfield, on the road to Chapel-en-le-Frith. Buses stop at Goose Green and there is a large car park.

Finishing Walk: There is a bus stop a short distance away from the pay kiosk at Chatsworth House car park. In addition, bus stops can be found on the road, close to the end of the drive up to Chatsworth House. To continue the walk, go to the Chatsworth House to Rowsley route section. Alternatively, you can return to Baslow along a different route using the instructions provided overleaf.

Walking in Chatsworth Park is available all year.

Terrain: Walk through parkland to one of the Treasure Houses of Great Britain, with an alternative return route if required.

Chatsworth Park's delightful little Cricket Ground, with its thatched roof, is a splendid place for a game of cricket.

Queen Mary's Bower, where Mary, Queen of Scots, once took her leisure.

The Route

1. From Goose Green walk to the right of the café, cross the packhorse bridge and turn right down a lane, past a group of thatched cottages. Continue in the same direction along the path to a kissing gate, designed to allow wheelchair access to Chatsworth Park.

2. After passing through the kissing gate, continue along the path in front of you, passing White Lodge and Chatsworth Cricket Club, to reach Queen Mary's Bower.

3. At this point you have a choice: turn right to continue the walk from Chatsworth to Rowsley, or turn left and walk towards Chatsworth House – the bus stop is at the top of the drive.

4. If you want to return to Baslow, follow the car park to the left, and where it ends take the higher of two roughly parallel roads. Continue with a fence close on your right, and where the fence bends to the right, maintain the same direction without deviating.

5. With a house in the distance on the right, where the road swings to the right, angle slightly to the left to go over a wooden platform stile and turn left down another access road.

6. After passing close to the Golden Gates, follow the perimeter of the field round to return to the kissing gate that you passed through earlier in the walk, from where you can retrace your steps to the start.

The Golden Gates at the Baslow end of Chatsworth Park.

15
Chatsworth House to Rowsley

The Walk

At the start of the walk it is worth taking a detour to visit Queen Mary's Bower, which is located only a few yards from the bridge leading to Chatsworth House. Here Mary, Queen of Scots, used to relax when she was held captive at Chatsworth.

There are lovely views of Chatsworth House and gardens as you walk along the banks of the Derwent. The 105-acre gardens were landscaped by Lancelot 'Capability' Brown, with the imposing Emperor Fountain the most impressive

Weir on the River Derwent at Chatsworth.

The walk through Chatsworth Park to Calton Lees provides a superb view of Chatsworth House.

Jasmine Cottage at Calton Lees, a riot of colour in the summer.

landmark. It was built in 1844 to impress Czar Nicholas of Russia. Unfortunately, the Czar was detained elsewhere and failed to visit Chatsworth. The fountain's single gravity-fed high spout rises to 290ft and is the tallest in Britain.

The hamlet of Calton Lees is quite beautiful in the summer, with its rich, honey-coloured stone cottages and stunning gardens. The cottages are tenanted by Chatsworth estate workers. It is always easy to recognise properties owned by the estate by the blue-painted doors.

Later in the walk there are striking views across the Derwent Valley of Beeley Moor. The moor is a wildlife sanctuary and is home to a wide range of birds. In spring or early summer you can see curlews and skylarks and many other birds. On the heather-clad moor, some 1,200ft above sea level, are over 30 prehistoric barrows and cairns. Hob Hurst's House is an unusual Bronze Age barrow that attracts a lot of attention. A small ring of five stones stands on a mound, surrounded by a rectangular bank and ditch. When the barrow was excavated in 1853, scorched human bones were found along with two pieces of lead ore. Various legends have sprung up, including one that refers to 'Hob' as a kindly goblin who made his home in this barrow and gave assistance to the local community.

Calton Lees Village is quite beautiful in the summer, with its rich, honey-coloured stone cottages and stunning gardens.

Horse and pony graze contentedly at Calton Lees, near the turn off for the walk to Rowsley.

As you walk down Church Lane into Rowsley, St Katherine's Church is passed. Inside the church is a fragment of a cross thought to be a ninth-century preaching cross. It is carved with braidwork and was found on the bed of the River Wye by two boys bathing in the 1900s. On the other side of the River Derwent, Paxton built an impressive Italianate railway station, now part of Peak Village, along with four stone cottages to house railway workers. The Station Hotel, renamed the Grouse and Claret, was built nearby and everything was ready to build a railway line through the valley. Unfortunately, there was a problem; the Duke of Devonshire was adamant that he would not allow the line to cross Chatsworth Park. If that was not bad enough,

the Duke of Rutland also refused an alternative plan for the railway to run across his estate at Haddon. All the railway company could do at the time was to run trains between Rowsley and Ambergate.

The problem was solved when the Duke of Rutland agreed to Midland Railway's plans to build a track out of sight in a cutting behind Haddon Hall. A new station was built a quarter of a mile south, and instead of the line running up the Derwent Valley, it ran along the Wye Valley. Paxton's splendid station was left isolated in the wrong valley. It was not until 1867 that the line finally reached Manchester.

The sign post points the way to Rowsley.

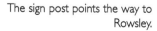

Walk Details

Length: 3 miles.

Start/Finish: Chatsworth House (SK259702) – Grouse and Claret Hotel, Rowsley.

Starting Walk: From the A6 take the B6012 road signed for Chatsworth House, from the Matlock to Buxton road. There are bus stops close to the car park at Chatsworth House and near the end of the drive. The car park at Chatsworth House is open to all during the visitor season. The car park at Calton Lees is open all year (Point 2).

Finishing Walk: The bus stop back to Chatsworth is on the B6012, between the entrance to Peak Village and the intersection with the A6. To continue the walk, go to the Rowsley to Darley Dale route section.

Terrain: Easy walking on well-trodden paths across fields and through parkland, with wonderful views of Chatsworth and the Derwent Valley. It can be muddy at most times of the year, particularly near Rowsley, so go prepared.

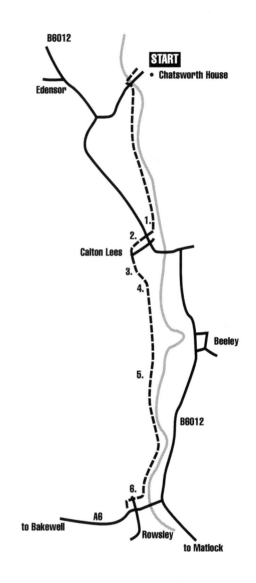

The Route

1. Walk away from Chatsworth House and over the bridge, turning left immediately to follow a path by the Derwent in front of the house. On reaching the ruins of an old mill, go to the right and cross the road to follow the path through the car park.
2. Where the car park ends, continue straight on for Calton Lees; the road soon curves to the right before dividing. Here you turn left, and where the houses finish, go over a stile on your left.

Rowsley is now only a short distance away.

3. Follow the path close to the wall on your left to within a few yards from the end of the field, go over a wooden-step stile and maintain the same direction in the next field, this time with the wall on your right.

4. At the end of the field, go over a stile set in a stone wall by a gateway and continue ahead, aiming for a gateway you can see in the distance.

5. Follow a well-trodden path, which gradually gets closer to the river, before running alongside it for a short distance and then angling slightly to the right to go over a stile and along a path through Bank Wood.

6. Go over a stile and across a field, with a wall close on your right, to reach a cart track. Follow the track to Rowsley, where you turn left down Church Lane. The Peacock Hotel is at the bottom of the lane on your left and, a few yards further on to the left, along the A6, is the Grouse and Claret Hotel.

Rowsley Post Office and store.

16
Beeley to Baslow Circular Walk

The Walk

An outstanding walk with excellent views and with Beeley, Chatsworth House, Baslow, Pilsley and Edensor all on the route. This walk could take a considerable amount of time to complete with so many fascinating places to explore.

From Beeley the path climbs up to Beeley Hilltop Farm, and then across the bracken-clad hillside on the edge of Beeley Moor to follow a woodland track, high above Chatsworth House and gardens.

Beeley Church and churchyard.

After passing both the Swiss Lake and the Emperor Lake, you arrive at the Hunting Tower. Elizabethan in construction, it has the most wonderful views over Chatsworth Estate and was used by the ladies of the House to view the hunt when it took place in the park below. The cannon at the base of the house came from a ship that fought at the battle of Trafalgar.

The route continues through Chatsworth Park, close to the banks of the River Derwent, passing the lovely little estate cricket ground on the way to Baslow.

What makes the village so beautiful is that almost all the farm and domestic buildings are built from the same honey-coloured stone.

The shortest of detours will take you to Baslow Church, where the tower clock displays 'Victoria 1897' on one side, instead of the usual numerals. Another surprise waits inside in the form of a dog whip in a glass case, supposedly to drive out stray dogs during service or, as has been suggested, to keep the congregation from snoring!

After leaving Baslow, the walk continues through fields before descending steeply to the A619 and then climbing sharply up through the attractive estate village of Pilsley. After a short walk towards Ballcross, a rough track leads down to Edensor. The splendid collection of differently designed houses makes you feel as if you're on a whistle-stop tour of Europe.

The view of the house and gardens as you walk across the park is unforgettable, even if the Emperor Fountain is not sending up jets of water nearly 300ft high.

The finger post sign indicates the path from Pig Lane to Beeley Hilltop.

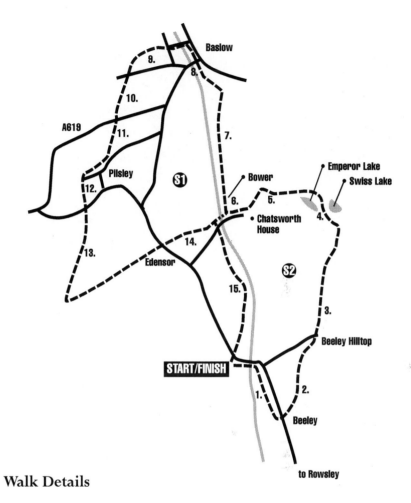

Walk Details

Length: 9.5 miles (Short Walk I – 5.5 miles, Short Walk II – 4.25 miles).

Start/Finish: Calton Lees car park (SK259683).

Starting/Finishing Walk: Leave the A6 south of Bakewell to join the B6012 to Chatsworth. The car park is on the left, 200 yards after crossing the bridge over the River Derwent. Buses stop at Chatsworth House (see Point 15).

Terrain: Good walking conditions, mainly using surfaced tracks and well-trodden field paths. There is some ascent to Beeley Moor and up to Pilsley, but nothing particularly strenuous. The long series of steps down from the Hunting Tower can be avoided by taking the slightly longer option and using the access track.

The Courtyard at Chatsworth House.

The Route

1. Depart along the road in front of the parking area, heading towards Chatsworth Garden Centre, but just before reaching it turn left down a woodland path that curves back to the B6012. Go to the right to the bridge over the river, where the traffic flow is controlled by traffic lights. Take care crossing the bridge, before immediately turning right to walk diagonally for three quarters of a mile across a long field to reach the B6012. Cross the road and walk up Church Lane, past St Anne's Church, turning to the left at the top, and within 30 yards take the stile on the right.

2. Walk up a short field to another stile, and in the next field continue straight ahead to the far left-hand top corner to go through a stile. Cross another field diagonally to a stile about 20 yards in from the top left-hand corner. Continue across a further field diagonally to a gate and walk along the track towards Beeley Hilltop Farm, with the wall close on the right. Follow the track as it swings round the farm buildings, where you turn left to a stile by a tyre dump on the right.

Chatsworth House seen from the bridge over the Derwent.

Picturesque houses at Edensor.

3. Once over the stile, turn left and within a few yards go over another stile onto the lane leading up to Beeley Moor. Go right and almost immediately left, over a stone-step stile angling to the right. Then go across a field to another stile, leading along the bracken-covered hillside. Follow the path up, keeping to the left at the top to go over a stone stile by a gate onto a woodland track.

4. Continue along the main track, keeping straight on at a track crossing point. The track bends first to the right and then to the left, before eventually passing Swiss Lake and the northern tip of Emperor Lake.

5. On reaching an electricity pole, turn left down a partly grassed track. In about 100 yards the Hunting Tower is passed and a short flight of steps descended to a service road. Turn left, and within a few yards start descending a long series of steps on the right. At the bottom of the steps, turn right onto a woodland track, passing an adventure playground on the left, to reach a stile by a gate into a field.

6. Follow the field round to the right to another stile, and then go to the left to join a parkland road and head towards Chatsworth House. From here walk down to the bridge over the River Derwent, but do not cross it.

7. Turn right alongside the river path and walk for about one mile, passing Chatsworth cricket ground with the Derwent only a short distance away on the left, until the park is departed through a swing gate designed to give access to wheelchair users.

8. After approximately 100 yards, go through a gate stile on the left, and within a short distance cross a narrow stone bridge. Walk across a field behind the Cavendish Arms to join a fenced path leading to the main road. Follow the road round to the left, and after crossing Devonshire Bridge turn right along Bubnell Road.

9. Directly opposite the Old Bridge go through a squeezer stile between two cottages and walk up a narrow path, before crossing three fields with the wall close on the right. In the next field, continue beside the wall for about 80 yards, before turning left where the wall

Party of walkers heading across Chatsworth Park.

turns sharply to the right. Walk straight across the field to a stile by a gate, leading onto a country lane.

10. Turn right along the lane and then, in about 50 yards, left into a field. Keeping close to the wall on the left, walk to the other end of the field and turn right without leaving the field. Just past the halfway point in the field, go over a stile in the wall close to a gate. Cross the field diagonally to the right as it drops down quite steeply to the road.

11. Go over the road by two stiles, and on the other side follow a steep track diagonally to the right to reach a stile in the corner. Turn left and walk alongside the wall to reach a minor road, where you go to the right and walk into the village of Pilsley.

12. Follow the road up a gentle slope past the Devonshire Arms, and at the end of the houses keep straight on along a rough track that soon swings to the left. Where the track ends, go over a stile and cross a field to another stile by a gate leading onto a road.

13. Cross over to the other side and continue up another road marked unsuitable for motors, and when it levels out, just before rising again, turn sharply left down a rough track leading to Edensor.

14. Leave the village by the main gates and cross the road to join a surfaced path that swings to the right and leads to the River Derwent.

15. Do not go over the bridge, but turn right alongside the river. Continue to follow the path by the Derwent in front of Chatsworth House and gardens until a derelict mill is reached. Here you turn right and walk up the slope to cross the road (B6012) to return to Calton Lees car park.

Short Walk I

Chatsworth House Walk (5.5 miles)

Route (From Chatsworth House {SK259702} – Chatsworth Park – Baslow – Pilsley – Edensor – Chatsworth House)

1. From the western side of Chatsworth House, where there is a car park and bus stop, walk down to the bridge over the River Derwent and follow the Beeley to Baslow circular route instructions from Point 7 to Point 14.
2. Cross the bridge and walk back to the starting point of the walk.

Edensor Church.

Short Walk II

Beeley Walk (4.25 miles)

Route (From Calton Lees {SK259683} – Beeley – Beeley Hilltop – Hunting Tower – Chatsworth House – Calton Lees)

1. From Calton Lees car park follow the Beeley to Baslow circular route instructions from Point 1 to Point 6, ignoring the last instruction and cross the bridge.

2. Once across the bridge, turn sharply left alongside the river and continue to follow the path by the Derwent in front of Chatsworth House and gardens, until a derelict mill is reached. Here you turn right and walk up the slope to cross the road (B6012) to return to Calton Lees car park.

Refreshment Stops

Stable Tea Rooms (Chapter 14/16) are situated in the former stables to Chatsworth House, which have been converted into a very impressive restaurant, tea rooms and shop complex. (Tel. 01246 582204)

Grouse and Claret (Chapter 15) at Rowsley, formerly the Station Hotel, but due to the demise of the railway it was renamed. It is a large, popular pub with a beer garden and children's play area. (Tel. 01629 733233)

Caudwell's Mill Tea Rooms (Chapter 15) are situated close to the River Wye at Rowsley. If it seems a little like sitting in church there is a reason: the seating and serving counter were salvaged from Crich Carr Chapel when it closed. (Tel. 01629 733185)

Places of Interest in the Locality

Chatsworth House, Garden, Farmyard and Adventure Playground, where visitors are free to wander in the magnificent grounds. The house stands in a deer park laid out by 'Capability' Brown in the 18th century, with hills and woods. There are shop and restaurant facilities available. The park is open all year. (Tel. 01246 582204)

Chatsworth Estate Farm Shop is situated at Pilsley, one and a half miles from Chatsworth House, at what used to be the stud farm and later became a milking parlour. Then in 1977 the Duchess of Devonshire opened the Farm Shop in the former tack room, which sells beef and lamb from the estate. As the shop has become more successful, it has expanded to include a whole range of products. Refreshment facilities are provided. Open daily. (Tel. 01246 582204)

Caudwell's Mill at Rowsley is powered by the River Wye and is the only complete Victorian working roller flour mill in the UK. There are a number of craft shops and a well-stocked gift shop, artist's gallery and café. (Tel. 01629 734374)

Peak Village is the Peak District's first and only factory outlet shopping centre, set in beautiful surroundings at Rowsley. Open every day. (Tel. 01629 735326)

Haddon Hall is perhaps the most perfect example of a medieval manor house in the country. The gardens are a delight and are believed to be the most romantic in Britain, being the setting for the elopement of Dorothy Vernon and John Manners. (Tel. 01629 812855)

17
Along the Derwent from Rowsley to Matlock – Sir Joseph Whitworth

The village of Rowsley stands at the junction of two valleys of the Rivers Derwent and Wye, with wooded hills on either side. It was the beauty of its setting in the 19th century which attracted artists, poets and anglers. Though the wonderful scenery remains relatively unspoilt and still attracts scores of visitors, a new attraction has arrived in recent years. The stylish Peak Village Shopping Complex, which successfully blends into the landscape, draws visitors to the village who want to shop and enjoy the lovely setting in which it stands.

An Anglo-Saxon settlement existed here before the Norman Conquest, and Rowsley is mentioned in the *Domesday Book* as an outlier of the Royal Manor of Bakewell. Nearby, on Stanton Moor and also on Beeley Moor, there is evidence of even earlier settlements in the form of stone circles and burial mounds, which date back at least to the Bronze Age. The oldest structure remaining in the village is the bridge over the Derwent, which was originally a 15th-century packhorse bridge before being widened.

Nowadays there are two Rowsleys, not surprisingly called Great and Little, but perhaps more unexpectedly it is the latter that has the larger population. Greater Rowsley is much the older part of the village and has a number of handsome buildings. The arrival of the railway in 1849 brought about the development of Little Rowsley.

Paxton built an impressive Italianate Railway Station, along with four stone cottages to house railway workers. The Station Hotel, now renamed the Grouse and Claret, was built nearby and everything was ready to extend the line through the valley. Unfortunately, this proved over optimistic and following objections an alterative route had to be found. The resited Rowsley Station was very popular with tourists and welcomed hundreds of visitors bound for Chatsworth. They usually completed their journeys by horse-drawn carriage.

The line was closed in 1967, but following the actions of a band of determined enthusiasts, who formed the Peak Railway Society, trains recommenced running from Matlock to Darley Dale Station in 1991. Six

Paxton's old station, now part of the Peak District Village Shopping Centre.

Caudwell's Mill information board at
entrance to the car park.

years later the line was extended to Rowsley
South Station. A journey on the train is an ideal
way to see the best of the valley and beat the
traffic jams, and you can even extend your
journey further. Indeed, only a short walk away
from the Peak Railway Station at Matlock you can
travel by rail from Matlock Station to London.

A mill has stood in the village since at least the
16th century. The latest, Caudwell's Mill, was
founded in 1874 and continued to operate for 104
years. When it closed a group of enthusiasts got
together to save what was the only complete
Victorian water turbine-powered roller mill in
the country. They had a fight on their hands as,
according to the Millers' Manual Association,
milling machinery no longer needed must be
destroyed to prevent reuse. After a lot of
persuasive talk, agreement was reached to waive
the ancient right and allow a small amount of
flour to be produced and the mill used for
exhibition purposes. Today, the mill continues to
operate alongside a busy craft centre and café.

Caudwell's Mill was founded in 1874
and continued to operate for 104
years. It is now run by a group of
enthusiasts.

Almost certainly the best-known building in
the village is the Peacock Hotel, with a stone
peacock sitting above the door. It was built in
1652 in Jacobean style by John Stevenson of
Elton, agent to the Manners Family, as a
gentleman's residence. It later served as a
farmhouse before it eventually became a hotel. In
its time it has housed many famous residents,
including royalty.

There are more small industrial companies
along the road from Rowsley to Matlock than in
any other part bordering the southern half of the
Peak District National Park. The industries are
mainly sited on the narrow band of land between
the A6 and the railway line. The railway, now
private and belonging to Peak Rail, only runs as
far as Rowsley South Station.

Peacock Hotel at Rowsey, with a stone
peacock sitting above the door. It was built
in 1652, in Jacobean style.

Peak Rail's Church Lane Crossing. The line was closed in 1967 but reopened by a group of enthusiasts.

The railway arrived in 1849 and Darley Dale soon expanded as a result, but in the 1960s the 'Beeching Axe' fell and the line from Matlock to Buxton closed. Peak Rail trains now steam along the old line between the road and river, but only as far as Rowsley South. The hoped-for extension to Buxton is now a forgotten dream.

Drivers and passengers who travel along the A6 see little of the beauty of the valley on their six-mile-long journey. Extensive ribbon development hides the view. The route is lined by rather sombre gritstone buildings and can become very congested at weekends and in the summer.

Darley Dale has had a town council since the late 1900s. It covers a wide area, including the old settlements of Hackney, Farley, Two Dales, Darley Hillside and Churchtown, as well as the piece along the A6. The council offices and meeting room are housed in the Whitworth Community Centre.

In 1849 the railway arrived, resulting in the expansion of Darley Dale, which became very much a railway village. Unfortunately, the line closed 119 years later. At its height it had been part of Midland Railway's line between Manchester Central and London St Pancras. Several years following the closure in 1967, steam trains recommenced running from Matlock to Darley Dale Station, and later to Rowsley South Station.

Stancliffe and Hall Dale quarries, on the northern side of the A6, provided flagstones for Trafalgar Square, Hyde Park Corner and the

Peak Rail extended the line to Rowsley South Railway Station in 1997.

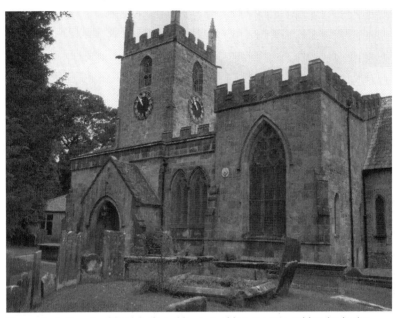

The ancient Church of St Helen's and its even older yew tree, said to be in the region of 2,000 years old.

Thames Embankment in London. Stone from the quarries was also used for many other notable buildings, including the Walker Art Gallery and St George's Hall in Liverpool. A standard gauge railway used to run from the quarries to the masonry yard and then onto the main railway line. Laid in 1903, it was taken up during World War One and transferred to France. It was relaid after the war and finally removed just before the outbreak of World War Two.

Red House Stables and Working Carriage Museum, situated a short distance from Matlock, is one of the Peak District's unique attractions. It holds one of the finest historic collections of horse-drawn vehicles and equipment in Britain. The present collection of carriages is almost priceless. It includes one of the very few surviving original hansom cabs, a stagecoach, a Royal Mail coach in full livery and two genuine Landaus, plus numerous other private and commercial vehicles. In addition, it is also a horse-riding and carriage-driving centre.

Darley Bridge was originally a 15th-century packhorse bridge, before being widened.

The river and path run close together as you approach Matlock.

Sir Joseph Whitworth

Sir Joseph Whitworth was born in Stockport, the son of Charles Whitworth, a teacher and Congregational minister. He became one of the great Victorian mechanical engineers, ranking alongside men such as George Stephenson, and I.K. Brunel. He was a manufacturer of machine parts, promoting absolute accuracy in measurement and the standardization of machine parts.

Whitworth's aptitude for mechanics became apparent when he served his apprenticeship at his uncle's cotton spinning mill at Ambergate. Later he went on to gain experience elsewhere, before setting up business in Manchester manufacturing machine parts. Most other engineers made machines for their own use which were not for sale. He is not known so much for his inventions as for his great ability to perfect existing ideas. His machines were very well designed, and were built to a high degree of accuracy, embodying ingenious devices of his own invention. He famously invented the Whitworth screw thread.

By 1851, it became clear that Whitworth was the foremost mechanical engineer of his day, when he won more awards than any other exhibitor at the Great Exhibition. When the Crimean War broke out two years later, he designed the Whitworth Rifle, which was far superior to the Enfield Rifle which was in use at that time.

Whitworth was responsible for much of the development at Darley Dale. He bought Stancliffe Hall in 1854 and had it virtually rebuilt but did not move in until 1871. A shy man, prone to disputes with other land owners, he built a high wall around Stancliffe Hall to protect his privacy. After his death his wife founded the Whitworth Institute, a community centre for Darley Dale residents, Whitworth Park with its many sports facilities, and Whitworth Hospital. Although not particularly popular during his lifetime, the people of the village erected an obelisk in Whitworth Park after his death, in recognition for all he had done for the community.

18
Rowsley to Darley Dale

The Walk

The first section of the walk follows the riverside path to Northwood, along a tree-lined route, which hides what is a busy industrial area serviced by the A6. After a short distance the Derwent is joined by the River Wye, one of its major tributaries. The walk through the woodland ends as it began, with industrial units very much in evidence.

In 1849 the railway arrived, resulting in the expansion of Darley Dale, which became a railway village. Unfortunately, the line closed 119 years later. At its height it had been part of Midland Railway's line between Manchester Central and London St Pancras. Rowsley Station was very popular with tourists and welcomed hundreds of visitors bound for Chatsworth. They usually completed their journeys by horse-drawn carriage

It only survived until 1968, when the line was closed and lifted. Fortunately, in 1975 a group of enthusiasts formed the Peak Railway Society with the aim of reopening the line. At first a Steam Centre was opened at Buxton, but later it was the southern end of the line where all the activity was concentrated. The undergrowth was hacked away and rails reinstated, and services recommenced between Matlock and Darley Dale in 1991.

The Grouse and Claret at Rowsley, one of the most popular pubs in the Derbyshire Dales.

Walking by the riverbank during the early
part of the walk.

Midland Railway information board. In 1975 a
group of enthusiasts formed the Peak Railway
Society to reopen the railway.

The line was extended to the site of the former
Rowsley locomotive depot, which saw its first
passenger trains in 1997 and further developments
are still ongoing. A journey on the train is an ideal
way to see the best of the valley and beat the traffic
jams, but is only available on a limited basis.

Churchtown was described accurately by an
18th-century writer as 'Churchtown, no town' as it
was only a small hamlet, and is not much bigger
today. It is dominated by the ancient Parish Church
of St Helen's and its even older yew tree, said to be
in the region of 2,000 years old. The mediaeval
church, which includes two Burne-Jones windows,
is large and impressive. A short distance along the
road, past the level crossing, is a church of a different
kind – the popular Church Inn.

Northwood Buffet on the Peak Railway line.

The line was reopened in 1997 to Rowsley South Station, by Peak Rail.

Darley Dale Cricket Club was formed in 1863 at its pretty riverside location near Darley Bridge. Cricket has always been a very popular game in Darley Dale, and an article in the *Daily Mail* on 17 March 1923 proclaimed, 'Darley Dale, a village of under 4,000 inhabitants, holds a unique position in English cricket – one resident in every 16 plays cricket.'

The cricket club converted in the 1960s from so-called 'friendly matches' to league cricket and joined the Nottinghamshire and Derbyshire Border League, which subsequently became the Derbyshire County League. The club had a very successful era during the 1970–80s, winning both league titles and cup finals several times. A notable date in the club's history was 7 September 1975, when over 6,000 people crammed into the ground to watch a televised John Player League match between Derbyshire and Hampshire.

Darley Dale lies in an attractive part of the Derwent Valley, on the edge of the Peak District between Matlock and Bakewell. It has had a town council since the late 1900s; the council offices and meeting room are housed in the Whitworth Community Centre. These are named after Sir Joseph Whitworth, who was a manufacturer of machine tools, promoting absolute accuracy in measurement and the standardization of machine parts. Whitworth's wife gave the large park located next to railway line to the inhabitants of Darley Dale after his death. The park won the 'Britain in Bloom' award in 2003, in the 'Large Village' category.

Walkers on the concessionary path by the railway line.

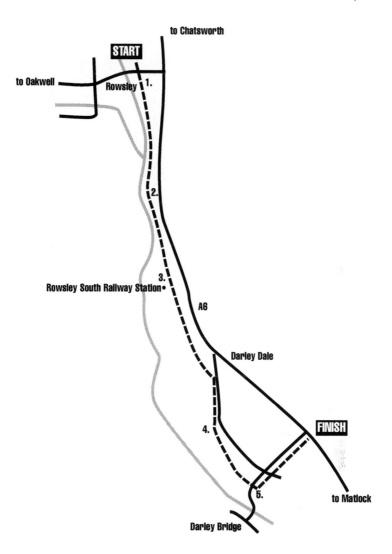

Walk Details

Length: 3 miles.

Start/Finish: Grouse and Claret Hotel, Rowsley (SK256659) – Darley Dale.

Starting Walk: Rowsley is on the A6 between Matlock and Bakewell. The Grouse and Claret Hotel faces the A6, where there are bus stops. As you enter the village from the east there is a

113

Church Inn at Churchtown, once referred to as 'Churchtown, no town' because of its size.

car park in Old Station Road, the first turn on the left, as the A6 bends to the left just after passing the Chatsworth turn. From the Bakewell direction it is the first turn right after crossing the river.

Finishing Walk: Walk up the B5057 to the A6. The bus stops are located at Broad Walk.

Terrain: Easy, flat walking through woodland, along quiet lanes and through meadows in this picturesque part of the valley.

The Route

1. From Rowsley walk in an easterly direction along the A6 and cross the bridge over the Derwent, turn right down Old Station Close (car park on the right). Go through a narrow gap to the right of the building at the end of the road to follow a concessionary path through trees, keeping close to the river.
2. Do not deviate from the main path until you reach a marker post, where you turn left and cross a plank bridge over a water course to gain access to a wide track running parallel with the river.
3. Continue along the track past Peak Rail's Rowsley Station. As the path narrows and the end railway shed is reached, go over a stile and follow the concessionary path by the railway line to a reach a minor road at Churchtown.
4. Turn right down the road and walk past St Helen's Church, immediately after the churchyard wall ends. Take the stile on the right and cross a field diagonally.
5. Go through a squeezer stile and turn left to walk close to the hedge side to reach Darley Dale Cricket Club. Walk along the access road to the B5057 and turn left to go up the road to Darley Dale and the A6. To continue the walk, turn right and follow the instructions for the Darley Dale to Matlock Walk.

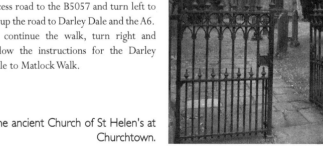

The ancient Church of St Helen's at Churchtown.

19
Darley Dale to Matlock

The Walk

At an early stage of this delightful walk, the Square and Compass Public House is passed. It is an attractive 18th-century pub, with the name boldly displayed on the roof as well as more conventionally on the front of the building. Only a short distance away is the 15th-century five-arched Darley Bridge.

Once across the bridge, the name Oaker is soon encountered, which gets its name from the Romans who mined lead in the vicinity. Oddly, the name changes later to Oker. The scenery remains beautiful along this stretch of the valley, especially the view of Oker Hill, immortalised by the

The Square and Compass at Darley Bridge. It also has its name on the roof.

Three Stags Head at Darley Bridge.

The lane leading from Darley Bridge.

poet William Wordsworth in his sonnet about the lone sycamore tree on the hillside. According to local legend, the poet had been on a visit to Dovedale, and on his return journey he was accommodated for the night at a cottage in Snitterton. From here he was able to look through the north-facing window towards the sycamore tree on the nearby hilltop, a view which inspired him to compose his sonnet.

The story goes that when two local brothers left the village to seek their fortune they each planted a sycamore tree. Sadly, the brothers quarrelled and parted company. Will, who stayed in the locality, flourished and prospered, while his brother, Tom, left and never returned, falling on hard times and passing away. At the same time his tree withered and died. For almost 200 years there has been a single Sycamore tree standing alone on the hillside.

Approaching Oker.

Oker can be seen in the distance on this valley bottom walk.

Approaching Matlock, the Peak Rail Station is passed near the new bypass of the centre of the town. Sainsbury's has been recently built and occupies the site of what was once Cawdor Quarry. A smart new bus station for buses heading north now stands by Matlock Railway Station, which was opened by the Manchester, Buxton, Matlock and Midlands Junction Railway in 1849. The station buildings were designed by Sir Joseph Paxton and the station now holds Grade II listed building status. At the time of writing it is a single platform terminus, but plans are in hand for the downside platform to become the new terminus for Peak Rail.

The development of Matlock owed much to the fact that it was on the main railway line between London and Manchester, with a branch line to Buxton. This came to an end on Saturday 29 June 1968, when services beyond Matlock were discontinued, as a result of Dr Beeching's cuts and the recent electrification of the West Coast route from London Euston to Manchester. The line to the south remained open and is still in use today, being regarded as one of the most scenic railway routes in England.

In 1893 Matlock opened a cable tramway, which was claimed to have the steepest gradient in the world. It ran from Crown Square up Bank Street.

Houses on the lane to Oker.

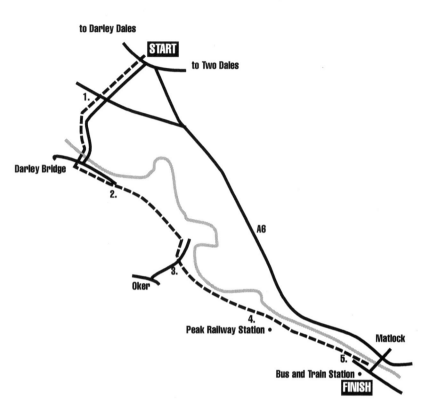

Walk Details

Length: 2.75 miles.

Start/Finish: A6 at Darley Dale (SK276629) on the Matlock to Rowsley road/Matlock Railway and Bus Station.

Starting Walk: At Darley Dale, close to the intersection with the B5057, to Darley Bridge and Winster road. Bus stops at Broad Walk on the A6, from where you walk down the B5057. Roadside car parking is available just off the A6.

Finishing walk: The bus station, which adjoins the railway station, takes northbound passengers. For those passengers going in the opposite direction, the bus stop is on Bakewell Road, which is found by crossing Matlock Bridge and turning left – the stop is on the right by the supermarket. The railway only takes southbound passengers.

Terrain: Easy, level walking, mainly along lanes and good paths.

Houses at Darley Bridge.

The Route

1. From Darley Dale walk down the B5057 past Darley Dale Cricket Club and the Square and Compass Public House, cross Darley Bridge, turning left once over the bridge signed for Oaker – Gated Road.

2. After coming to the end of the houses continue along the road, which eventually bends to the right and gently starts to climb up towards Oker (the more usual spelling).

3. Walk past a bungalow and in front of the next one, turn left down a narrow path between hedges to reach a field at the bottom.

4. Maintain the same direction through three fields, with the river close on your left. At the bottom corner of the third field, go over a stile onto a rough track, running close to the Derwent.

5. Continue along the track, passing an industrial site and going under the recently constructed bridge for the bypass, which takes traffic along the A6. On reaching Matlock Bridge, cross the road and turn right for the railway/bus station (northbound). To continue the walk, follow the instructions for the Matlock to Matlock Bath Walk.

The walk close to the River Derwent coming into Matlock.

20
Matlock to Rowsley Circular Walk

The Walk

This is a lovely walk with superb views of the Derwent and Wye valleys. The first part of the walk from Matlock follows the river valley. After leaving Darley Bridge, however, you climb up steadily to Stanton Moor, before descending through the fields to Rowsley and returning to Matlock, close to the Peak Railway line.

Stanton Moor is an isolated gritstone outcrop in the heart of limestone country and is one of the richest prehistoric sites in Derbyshire. It is famous for its Bronze Age relics – the best known is the Nine Ladies Stone Circle. Legend has it that the nine ladies danced here on the Sabbath Day and were turned to stone as a punishment, along with the fiddler who stands nearby. Last century the Heathcote family excavated in excess of 70 burial mounds on the moor.

Stone quarrying has been an important industry in the area over a long period and provided employment for many Stanton people. Towards the end of the 19th century, out of a population of 717 there were 103 quarry workers. The whole subject of quarrying in such a beautiful area is now a very contentious subject.

On the edge of Stanton-in-Peak your route takes you past the local cricket ground, which must have one of the prettiest views in the country. 'The Stand', which is passed on the walk

Darley Bridge, originally a packhorse bridge before widening.

National Trust sign at Stanton Moor Edge.

along the Stanton to Rowsley road, is an excellent place to get a magnificent panoramic view over the beautiful Wye Valley. Originally known as 'The Belvedere', it is a viewing platform with a stone seat, built by the Thornhill family of Stanton Hall.

Continuing on your journey down the hillside, you go through the tiny hamlet of Congreave. This is where rabbits used to be reared for the Haddon Hall tables, the name 'Congreave' meaning 'rabbit hole'. The walk then levels out and follows the beautiful River Wye to Rowsley.

Rowsley is well worth exploring, and Caudwell's Mill and Craft Centre in particular should not be missed. Another highlight on the return journey is the ancient Parish Church of St Helen's and its even older yew tree, said to be in the region of 2,000 years old, which dominate the small hamlet of Churchtown.

Beautiful views over the Wye Valley open up as the walk progresses.

Stone quarrying has been an important industry in the area over a long period, but is a contentious subject.

The final stages of the walk follow the Peak Railway line, brought back to life by the actions of a band of determined enthusiasts. Trains recommenced running from Matlock to Darley Dale Station in 1991, and six years later the line was extended to Rowsley South Station.

Approaching Rowsley with the River Wye only just out of view.

Stanton-in-the-Peak Cricket Club, is situated in a stunning location.

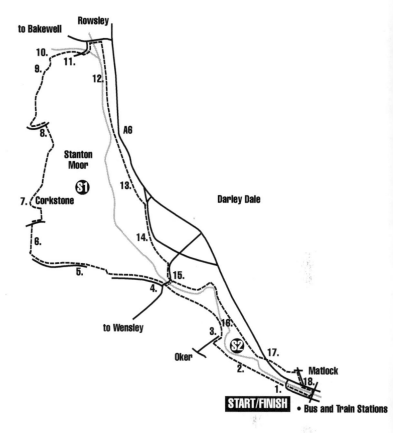

Walk Details

Length: 12.5 miles (Short Walk I – 7.5 miles, Short Walk II – 5 miles).

Start/Finish: Matlock Bridge (SK 297602).

Starting/Finishing Walk: The bus station at Matlock Bridge, which adjoins the railway station, takes northbound passengers. For those passengers going in the opposite direction, the bus station is on Bakewell Road, which is found by crossing Matlock Bridge and turning left – the station is on the right, by the supermarket. The railway only takes southbound passengers. A pay and display car park is only a few yards away.

Terrain: An attractive walk along quiet country lanes and through fields to Darley Bridge. A slow, steady ascent gradually leads to Stanton Moor. The views from the moor and the descent towards the River Wye are outstanding. There are a few short, steep ascents and descents on this walk.

The Route

1. Take the riverside path from Matlock Bridge, which is virtually opposite the railway and new bus station (northbound) and close to the pay and display car park. The path leads you along the banks of the River Derwent, under the bypass and past Peak Railway Station. Later you walk by the works of the Permanite Asphalt Products Division.

2. After crossing a stile into a field the path soon divides; keep to the right, close to the river. Continue straight ahead to cross two further fields and then walk up an enclosed path to reach Ashton Lane.

3. Turn right down the lane and follow it round, ignoring a possible left turn, as it gradually bends to the left. Continue first through fields and then past houses to reach Darley Bridge.

4. From here follow the road round to the left for approximately 100 yards, before going to the right up Oldfield Road. At a fork in the road, go to the left and follow it uphill until it bends sharply to the right, when you continue straight up a rough cart track by Cowley Knowl.

5. Continue ahead along Clough Lane, a farm access track, for nearly one mile, before turning right at a footpath junction. Walk up a field and the down another one, keeping close to the boundary fence on the left.

6. Follow the waymarked route past Barn Farm Holiday Cottages to go through a yard, and walk up the right-hand side of the field ahead to join a clear path through woodland. On reaching a minor road, turn right and then left in about 40 yards onto Stanton Moor.

7. At a fork in the main track go to the left and then turn right along a clear path, near to the Cork Stone. Proceed across the moor to the Nine Ladies Stone Circle, leaving the moor by angling to the left along a path that takes you to a minor road, where you turn left.

8. Follow the road downhill through woodland towards Stanton-in-Peak. At the end of the wood turn right at a fingerpost sign, heading past a cricket ground and through a wood, keeping to an obvious path near the edge of the woodland.

9. On reaching a minor road turn right, and after a short distance go to the left down a steeply descending field, angling at about 45 degrees to the right to go over a stile midway up the field. Keep to the right in the next field to cross a stile by a water trough.

10. Turn left down a steep and narrow lane leading to Congreave. Turn right at a footpath sign opposite Dovehouse Farm and after a few yards you enter a field by a stile. Follow the path to the right as it leads round the base of the hill to a stile in the corner.

11. Go through a small wood and cross the next field, angling slightly to the right towards a line of trees, to join a green farm track. Continue along the track to a stile to gain access to the road and turn left towards Rowsley. Follow the road round to reach the A6 opposite the Peacock Hotel and turn right.

12. Continue along the A6 from the Peacock Hotel, cross the bridge over the Derwent and turn right down Old Station Close (car park on the right). Go through a narrow gap to the right of the building at the end of the road to follow a concessionary path through trees, keeping close to the river. Do not deviate from the main path until you reach a marker post, where you turn left and cross a plank bridge over a water course to gain access to a wide track running parallel with the river.

13. Continue along the track past Peak Rail's Rowsley Station. As the path narrows and the end railway shed is reached, go over a stile and follow the concessionary path by the railway line to a reach a minor road at Churchtown.

View over Stanton-in-Peak.

14. Turn right down the road and walk past St Helen's Church, immediately after the churchyard wall ends. Take the stile on the right and cross a field diagonally. Go through a squeezer stile and turn left to walk close to the hedge side to reach Darley Dale Cricket Club. Walk along the access road to the B5057. Turn right and walk down the road past the Square and Compass Public House.

15. Take the path between the pub and the bridge. There are two choices and you need to follow the path on the right by Flatts Farm. This path leads you along the right-hand side of a wall, through two fields, before turning left and heading diagonally across another field to a stile.

16. From this point, follow the obvious route to gain access to the Peak Railway; do not cross the line, but walk to the right by the fence. Continue along the permissive path by the line for approximately one mile. Then, with the A6 about 50 yards away on the left and the river close by on the right, go through a wide metal gate, cross the track and pass through a wooden gate.

17. Walk up a short path, cross the A6 and turn right. After a few yards take the surfaced path leading uphill on the left; the fingerpost sign is to the rear of the bus shelter. Keep on the path over the top of a cul-de-sac and then an estate road, turning right when you reach a road called Hurts Hollow, and continue down Dimple Road.

18. On reaching the bottom of the road, turn left along the A6 and follow the road towards the centre of Matlock, past the bus station for southbound passengers. Go to the right across Matlock Bridge and over the River Derwent. Once over the bridge, turn right for the railway (southbound only), bus stations for northbound passengers and the car park.

Calton Lees.

Short Walk I

Rowsley Walk (7.5 miles)
Route (From Rowsley {SK256659} – Churchtown – Darley Bridge – Stanton Moor –
Stanton-in-Peak –Rowsley)

1. Follow the Rowsley to Matlock circular route instructions from Point 12 to Point 14.
2. After walking past the Square and Compass Public House, cross the bridge over the River Derwent and turn right.
3. From this point follow the Rowsley to Matlock circular route instructions from Point 4 to Point 11.

Short Walk II

Darley Bridge Walk (5 miles)
Route (From Darley Bridge {SK270620} – Peak Railway – Matlock – Oker – Darley Bridge)

1. Cross Darley Bridge and, with the Square and Compass Public House in front of you, take the right-hand path of two paths by Flatts Farm and follow the Rowsley to Matlock circular route instructions from Point 15 to Point 18, but do not cross the road.
2. After crossing Matlock Bridge, take the riverside path, which is virtually opposite the railway and new bus station (northbound) and close to the pay and display car park.
3. Follow the Rowsley to Matlock circular route instructions from Point 1 to Point 3.

Refreshment Stops

Square and Compass (Chapter 18/20) is an attractive 18th-century pub overlooking Darley Bridge, midway between Darley Dale and Wensley. Surprisingly, the name is also displayed on the roof tiles. (Tel. 01629 733255)

Regent House Tea Rooms (Chapter 19/20) is situated on Dale Road, a short distance south of the rail/bus station at Matlock. A good selection of speciality teas and coffees are provided, plus a wide range of hot and cold meals. (Tel. 01629 583660)

Crown Hotel (Chapter 19/20) in Crown Square, Matlock, close to the bus station (southbound), is a popular pub in the JD Wetherspoon chain. (Tel. 01629 580991)

Places of Interest in the Locality
Rowsley to Matlock

Peak Rail is a preserved railway, operating steam trips from Matlock Riverside Station to Rowsley South, calling at Darley Dale. Normally rides are available on Sundays throughout the year. Trains usually operate on Saturdays from April to October and midweek in the peak season. A number of special event days are held every year. (Tel. 01629 580381)

Red House Stables and Working Carriage Museum at Darley Dale holds one of the finest collections of original horse-drawn vehicles and equipment in Britain. The collection includes one of the very few remaining hansom cabs, a stagecoach, a Royal Mail coach and many others. (Tel. 01629 733583)

St Helen's Parish Church at Churchtown is particularly famous for its yew tree, which is said to be in the region of 2,000 years old. 'Churchtown, no town', as it was once described by an 18th-century writer, was only a small hamlet in the 18th century and is not much bigger today.

The Old Market Hall at Winster dates back to the 17th century when the village was granted the right to hold a market. It became the first National Trust property in Derbyshire and the Peak District in 1906 and it is now used as an exhibition and information centre.

Well at Rowsley, opposite the Peakcock Hotel, it is dressed for the village Well Dressings.

21
The Matlocks – John Smedley

Scenically, Matlock, or 'The Matlocks' as they should more correctly be called, is the most attractive town in Derbyshire. Much of it lies in a deep gorge, with dramatic scenery in all directions, along which rushes the busy A6, with the River Derwent never far away. The railway is left to tunnel through the sheer limestone cliffs.

Originally a string of small settlements, it was not until the discovery of medicinal springs in Matlock Bath at the end of the 17th century that much attention was paid to the area. Matlock Bath gradually became fashionable with the wealthy in the 18th century, but its development was limited by its somewhat inaccessible location.

The arrival of the railway in 1849 with cheap fares changed its character, putting it within easy affordable reach for day trippers, who flocked there from Nottingham and Derby. The large crowds attracted touts, who hung about the streets trying to persuade customers to see the sights, and it was not long before the wealthy moved on in search of a more peaceful setting. Many of them only went the short distance to Matlock Bank, where John Smedley was just setting up his hydropathy. Smedley died in 1874, but the business continued to prosper, as did a number of other similar establishments on Matlock Bank.

As the number of visitors increased, so did the demand for shops and services, and Matlock Bridge became a lively shopping centre. Hydropathy continued to flourish and the town to grow until World War One, but after the war the number of hydropathic establishments began to dwindle. The empty buildings were converted into hotels, guesthouses, schools and training establishments. Only Smedley's and Lilybank reopened after World War Two and struggled on for a while before both of them closed. Smedley's Hydro is now the home of Derbyshire County Council.

Hall Leys Park with the bandstand in the background.

The former tram shelter that used to stand in Crown Square is now located in Hall Leys Gardens.

The development of Matlock owed much to the fact that it was on the main railway line between London and Manchester. This came to an end in 1967, when the line north of the town was closed. Now Peak Rail provides scenic rail trips, mainly steam-hauled, to a new station at Rowsley South, a round trip of eight miles. At Matlock station, the stationmaster's house is attributed to Sir Joseph Paxton, who landscaped the gardens at Chatsworth and was the creator of Crystal Palace.

Pedestrian bridge in Hall Leys Gardens showing heights of recent floods.

Matlock is famous for another line – a cable tramway line claimed to have the steepest gradient in the world. It opened in 1893 and ran for nearly a mile from Crown Square, up Bank Street to the top of Rutland

Riber Castle looking down on Matlock, which was built by John Smedley.

Matlock Bridge, where the river was originally forded.

Street. Job Smith, who was the owner of Malvern House Hydro on Smedley Street, was instrumental in bringing the tramway to Matlock. He had seen the steep tramway in San Francisco in operation and thought that something similar would be ideal for Matlock, conveying visitors back and forth from the town centre.

Finance was raised principally through Sir George Newnes, who, when the company ran into financial difficulties, bought it and gave it to the town. It continued to carry passenger's

uphill for twopence and down for one penny until mounting costs caused it to close in 1927. The tram shelter from Crown Square has been relocated into Hall Leys Park, and the tram house still stands at the top of Rutland Street. Many people in recent years, when toiling up Bank Street, must have wished that the tramway still operated.

Sir George Newnes, born in 1851 in Matlock Bath where his father was vicar, went into publishing as a representative in his early 20s. One day, when he was reading aloud bits from the newspaper, he hit on the idea of publishing a paper that contained nothing other than 'titbits', as he called them.

Matlock Bath rising steeply upwards to the Heights of Abraham.

Matlock Bath is a premier meeting place for motorcyclists.

He raised the money to get started by buying and selling a restaurant. When *Titbits* was published it was a great success; the inclusion of competitions for prizes was a masterstroke. Among the many popular magazines he started were *The Strand*, *WideWorld Magazine*, *Review of Reviews* and *Country Life*. He was a great philanthropist and, apart from giving the cable railway to the people of Matlock, he made many other bequests, including one to the cliff railway at Lynton in Devon.

Matlock Bridge is the area where most of the shops were originally situated. The bridge itself started life as a packhorse crossing to replace the ford. Dale Road was once considered one of the most elegant shopping streets in the East Midlands. To the rear are pleasant riverside walks and Hall Leys Park, where excellent recreational facilities for young and old are available.

At the head of the park is the ornate tram shelter that once stood in Crown Square; there is also a refreshment room and bandstand. From here are excellent views of the ruins of Riber Castle, built and lived in by John Smedley until his death. It was bought in 1962 by a group of zoologists, who created a 60-acre fauna reserve and rare breeds centre. Unfortunately, it closed in 2000.

The original settlement of Old Matlock sits on the hillside to the east of the Derwent. There has been a church here since the 12th century, and a tablet in St Giles Church recalls a remarkable union between Adam and Grace Woolley, whose marriage lasted for nearly 76 years – surely a record for those days. At Matlock Green on the A515 a fortnightly cattle market used to be held, dating back to 1880. A public house existed on the site from the 17th century and May Fairs used to be held there.

Matlock Bath attracts most visitors; a busy little place well stocked with gift shops, cafés and amusements. But its spectacular views are what are most admired, as anyone who has gazed at the view from a good vantage point on either side of the narrow gorge can confirm. It is a popular haunt for serious rock climbers, who test their ability against the sheer rock face of High Tor. A much easier way to climb is to take the cable car up to the Heights of Abraham, named after General Wolfe's famous assault on Quebec.

The fascinating Peak District Mining Museum is housed in The Pavilion at Matlock Bath, and up on the hillside is the popular Gulliver's Kingdom. Here, children and their parents can spend many a happy hour in delightful wooded surroundings. The old Matlock Bath hydro now plays host to an aquarium.

Matlock Bath is the home of the Peak District Mining Museum.

The Fishpond Hotel Matlock Bath.

There are caves to explore and lovely riverside walks to enjoy, but the highlight of the year are the Illuminations and Venetian Nights, when decorated boats amid a myriad of bright lights ply their way slowly up and down the river.

John Smedley

John Smedley has been described as the man who made Matlock. He left school at the age of 14 and took a keen interest in his father's cotton mill at Lea, which was in serious financial trouble at the time. For 15 years he worked day and night until financial worries were a thing of the past. Having established himself, he married Caroline Harward, only to be struck down with a fever while on honeymoon in Switzerland. He recovered from the fever, but it left him feeling severely depressed and listless; all the usual medicinal treatments were tried but to no avail.

At last in desperation he turned to Dr McLeod, of whom he had heard good reports and went to his hydropathic clinic at Ben Rhydding, near Ilkley in Yorkshire. He came back home revitalised and determined to share his good fortune with others. All his employees were forced to undergo the water treatment, whether they were ill or not! Nor did he stop there, but started to offer the treatment to outsiders at his own house. When in 1851 Ralph Davis opened a small hydropathy on Matlock Bank, Smedley acted as his medical adviser.

In 1853 he bought the business from Davis and immediately started to expand. He built the Hydro, commonly known as Smedley's Hydro, to his own design, which soon catered for more than 2,000 patrons per year. Victorian times were full of rich people prepared to pay two guineas a week to live austerely in gracious surroundings.

The treatment prescribed consisted of regular applications of water, by wet sheets, sponges, bath or douches. Diet was carefully controlled and alcohol and tobacco were forbidden. Exercise was carefully monitored to ensure over fatigue was not caused on long walks and other strenuous exercises. Guests began their day at six in the morning and ended it at ten at night. Fines were imposed if rules were broken. Far from being put off by this kind of treatment guests loved it and kept coming back for more.

Smedley died in 1874, but the business continued to prosper, as did a number of other similar establishments on Matlock Bank. A guidebook published in 1898 lists more than 30 hydropathic establishments in Matlock.

Looking along Matlock Bath's main street from the south.

22
Matlock to Matlock Bath

The Walk

Scenically, Matlock, or 'The Matlocks' as they should more correctly be called, is the most attractive town in Derbyshire. Much of it nestles in a deep gorge, with dramatic scenery in all directions, along which rushes the busy A6, with the River Derwent never far away. The railway is left to tunnel through the sheer limestone cliffs.

The impressive limestone gorge cut by the river as it flows between Matlock and Matlock Bath has been described as one of the most spectacular natural features in Derbyshire. Apart from nature, man's influence on the gorge has been considerable, with the extraction of the rich mineral deposits being

High Tor Grounds.

Donkeys resting in a field by the side of the route to High Tor.

Superb views of the valley between Matlock and
Matlock Bath.

Sheer Drop warning notice, the fenced viewing
points provide magnificent views.

mined over the centuries. The Peak District Mining
Museum at Matlock Bath provides an excellent
opportunity for present-day visitors to learn what life
was like in those long ago days.

The area around Matlock Bridge is where most of the
shops are situated. Dale Road, on the southern side of the
station, was once considered one of the most elegant
shopping streets in the East Midlands.
The bridge itself started life as a
packhorse crossing to replace the ford.

At the head of the park is the ornate
tram shelter that once stood in Crown
Square; there is also a refreshment room
and bandstand. From here are excellent
views of the ruins of Riber Castle, built
and lived in by John Smedley until his

The A6 seen winding through the
valley from High Tor.

Cable cars crossing the valley to the Heights of Abraham.

death. It was bought in 1962 by a group of zoologists, who created a 60-acre fauna reserve and rare breeds centre. Unfortunately, it closed in 2000.

The walk through Hall Leys Park, recently refurbished, provides a pleasant riverside stroll. A short distance after entering the park, on the stone pillars by the footbridge are marked the flood heights in 1960 and 1965. The climb up High Tor is quite steep, but you are amply rewarded with superb views, but there is need to take care and not go near the edge as there is a 350ft drop. The path is easy to follow and there are superb views from the fenced viewing points.

During the 19th century a network of paths was constructed across High Tor to enable visitors to enjoy the spectacular views. The Pleasure Grounds themselves were laid out on High Tor in Victorian times by Frederick Charles Arkwright, and the path to the summit was appropriately named Arkwright's Grand Walk. A much-loved landmark on the walk over High Tor used to be the distinctive wooden refreshment hut, which is remembered by so many visitors. Unfortunately, it was burnt down in the 1990s.

Later on the walk the Heights of Abraham can be seen. In the summer cable cars glide back and forth, taking visitors to the top of the Pleasure Grounds on the opposite side of the gorge. When Queen Victoria visited Matlock Bath in 1844, she ascended the Heights of Abraham on a donkey. Visitors usually had to take the more strenuous option and walk, until the cable cars started to operate in 1984.

The Swiss-style station building was designed in this style to reflect the description given to the area: the 'Switzerland of England'.

Walk Details

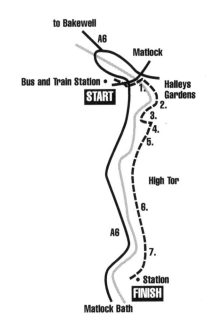

to Bakewell

A6

Matlock

Bus and Train Station •

START

Halleys Gardens

1.
2.
3.
4.
5.

High Tor

6.

A6

7.

• Station

FINISH

Matlock Bath

Length: 1.5 miles.

Start/Finish: Matlock Railway/Bus Station (SK297602) — Matlock Bath Railway Station.

Starting Walk: Off the A6 at Matlock, the station is a few yards on the left, beyond the bridge over the Derwent. Cars can be parked in the nearby pay and display car park. The bus station for passengers heading north is by the Railway Station, and for those going south it is on Bakewell Road.

Finishing Walk: A regular train service is available from Matlock Bath and buses run from stops on the A6, where you turn right after leaving the station (southbound 30 yards, northbound 150 yards), also buses leave from opposite the Fishpond Hotel/Peak District Lead Mining Museum. To continue the walk, go to Matlock Bath to Cromford route section.

Houses line the roadside on the approach to Matlock Bath.

High Tor, a popular spot for rock climbers to test their skills.

Terrain: Good, surfaced paths all the way and superb views from the fenced viewing points, but with a steep ascent and descent of High Tor. **Warning** – Keep to the path and do not walk close to the unprotected cliff edge, and ensure that children and animals are supervised at all times.

The Route

1. Follow the road round to the right from the station area to the A6 and turn left over Matlock Bridge towards the town centre.
2. Once over the bridge, go to the right into Hall Leys Park and continue along the path by the river, keeping straight on along an access road to 'Old Matlock' for 50 yards after leaving the park.
3. Go to right at a fingerpost sign, cross a footbridge, turn right and follow the river round, with Pic Tor rising steeply above on your left.
4. Pass under a railway bridge and when you arrive at a T-junction of paths, turn left under a bridge and walk up a steep, paved path.
5. As the path flattens out, with houses in front of you, turn sharp right at the sign for the High Tor Grounds and follow a rough track that ascends steadily to the summit. Ensure that you take care to observe the many warning notices about keeping well clear of the cliff edge.

Visitors waiting to board the cable cars.

6. At an information board for High Tor Matlock Bath Entrance go to the right and follow the path round, avoiding the path signed for Giddy Edge – dangerous in wet weather and for those who do not have a very good head for heights.
7. The path follows an obvious route as it descends steeply down several flights of somewhat uneven steps. At the bottom of the hill, the cable car station is passed and you bear left, close to the railway line, to reach Matlock Bath Railway Station and the town centre.

Cable Cars awaiting departure.

23
Matlock Bath to Cromford

The Walk

Nestling beneath limestone cliffs, with the River Derwent flowing below, in a beautiful wooded valley is the popular tourist centre of Matlock Bath. The town has been a tourist attraction since visitors first came to bathe in the thermal waters.

The name Matlock Bath, in fact, dates from the establishment of the first bath in the late 1690s. It was little more than a stone structure filled by a thermal spring, with a constant temperature of 68 degrees Fahrenheit. As the number of visitors who came to benefit from the medicinal qualities of the warm spring water increased, some development to improve the facilities took place.

Matlock Bath's beautiful scenery was compared to that of Switzerland and, together with the thermal qualities of the water, added to the attraction of the area. Facilities started to improve and the visits made by Queen Victoria, in 1832 and 1844, improved its reputation further.

Superb views are guaranteed on the first section of this short walk at any time of the year, but are best on a sunny day when the trees are not in full leaf. A word of warning: the steep descent through Hagg Wood can be slippery in wet weather and positively dangerous after frost.

The highlights of the year are the Illuminations and Venetian Nights, which start in early September and continue until the end of October. The riverbanks, decorated by illuminated

Matlock Bath's Swiss Style Railway Station. The Victorians referred to Matlock Bath as 'Little Switzerland'.

Housed in the Grand Pavilion is the Peak District Mining Museum, the only one of its kind in the world.

displays, and the floodlit cliffs, offer a truly memorable show. The climaxes of the Venetian Nights, on Saturdays and Sundays, are when decorated boats, with coloured lights twinkling, glide down the river; a magical experience enjoyed by people of all ages.

Housed in the Grand Pavilion is the Peak District Mining Museum, the only one of its kind in the world. It tells the story of lead mining from Roman to recent times in an interesting and innovative manner, with climbing shafts and tunnels providing a real insight into what working down a lead mine was really like.

Masson Mill was built in 1783 and was the only Arkwright mill to use the River Derwent,

which provided a power source 10 times greater than his first mill at Cromford. It now houses a shopping village on four floors, a restaurant and a working textile museum.

When Sir Richard Arkwright died, he was buried at St Giles Church at Matlock. Later his body was exhumed and reburied under

Gulliver's Kingdom in a woodland setting on the western side of the valley.

The main street in Matlock Bath.

the chancel at the Church of St Mary that his son had built near to Willersley Castle. The church was opened and became a parish church in 1797.

The French chateau-style station at Cromford, which has recently been renovated, is particularly worth seeing, even if you are not using the train. It was designed by G.H. Stokes, the son-in-law of Paxton. Probably due to its unusual character, a photograph of the station was used on the cover of the Oasis single *Some Might Say*.

Matlock Bath Rowing Boats, where the highlight of the year are the Venetian Nights.

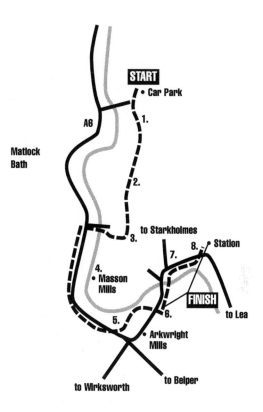

Walk Details

Length: 1.75 miles.

Start/Finish: Matlock Bath Railway Station (SK298586) – Cromford/Railway Station.

Starting Walk: The railway station is on the north side of Matlock Bath, just off the A6, by a large pay and display car park. There are bus stops on either side of the main road, opposite the Peak District Mining Museum/Fishpond Hotel and just north of the railway station turn-off.

Finishing Walk: A regular train service is available from Cromford and buses run from stops on the A6 close to the crossroads – turn left at the cross roads to go north, and turn right to go south. To continue the walk, go to the Cromford to Whatstandwell route section.

Terrain: A steady climb at the start of the walk with a steep descent to the River Derwent, which can be very slippery in wet weather and dangerous in frosty conditions. The remainder of the walk is flat and easy.

Pick-up truck adverting the museum at Masson Mill, which is also home to a retail shopping complex.

The Route

1. From the railway station car park walk through the coach park to join a path rising up above the River Derwent.

2. The path climbs steadily close to the fence to the top of the cliff. Continue along the cliff path as far as you can go, before going down the path on the right.

3. The trail now descends quite steeply along an uneven, stepped path in a zigzag fashion through Hagg Wood. On reaching the river, walk to the right and cross New Bridge.

4. Turn right into Derwent Pleasure Gardens and continue your walk along the riverbank, before going to the left to reach the A6. Turn left along the road and walk along the A6, past Arkwright's, Masson Mill.

5. Shortly after passing the mill, before reaching the road junction turn left (Cromford village is to the right, at the crossroads) along a concessionary path running between Scarthin Rock and the River Derwent.

Masson Mill was built in 1783 and was the only Arkwright mill to use the River Derwent.

6. If you have time, take a detour and follow the path leading off to the right to visit Arkwright's Mills (to catch the bus after you have finished exploring, walk up Mill Road to the A6), returning later to the same place to continue your walk towards St Mary's Church.

7. On reaching the road, maintain the same direction, crossing the bridge and keeping to the footpath, ignoring the left turns to Willersley Castle and Starkholmes.

8. Just as the road starts to bend to the right, go in the opposite direction up the road to Cromford Railway Station.

24
Matlock to Cromford Circular Walk

The Walk

As you pass through Hall Leys Park at an early stage in the walk, the notice on the footbridge over the river shows the level of floods in past years. Flood-prevention measures appear to have alleviated this problem in recent years.

The climb up to High Tor is quite steep, but you are rewarded with excellent views. At the first clifftop view point there are some picnic tables and railings at the cliff edge. Regular safety notices instruct walkers to keep to the path and to supervise children and animals at all times. On the descent you pass the cable car station for the Heights of Abraham. Opened in 1984, it was the first Alpine-style cable car ride in Great Britain.

The six-storeyed middle section of Masson Mill, on the A6, was erected by Sir Richard Arkwright in 1783–84. The chimney and some other buildings on the north side and the newer buildings on the south side were built at a later date by the English Sewing Company.

The Exit from High Tor at Matlock Bath. Pleasure Grounds were laid out on High Tor in Victorian times.

After passing through Cromford Market Place, the route takes you up Scarthin, a former lead-mining settlement. Behind the Boat Inn is a large pond originally used to store water for Arkwright's Cotton Mills. Although Masson Mill was powered by water from the River Derwent, Arkwright's Mills at Cromford used a complicated system of dams and water courses, drawing water from the Bonsall Brook and Cromford Sough.

The path climbs up the hillside above Scarthin, with the Via Gellia, a steep-sided wooded 'dry' valley, increasingly becoming a

The steep descent to the river at Matlock Bath to the eastern bank of the Derwent.

Jubilee Bridge 1887 at Matlock Bath. A second bridge further to the south is now in place.

distant view. The road was cut through thick woodland by Philip Gell of Hopton Hall in the 1790s. Its purpose was to enable lead from his mines to be transported more easily to the smelter and to Cromford Canal Wharf. The unusual name arose from the Gell family's belief that they were descended from the Romans. The fabric known as Viyella is named after the valley where it was originally produced, near to the turn-off for Bonsall.

The ancient former lead-mining village of Bonsall was once described by the *Daily Mail* as 'the healthiest village in England' because of the long lifespans of its inhabitants, who were kept fit by climbing its long streets. From The Pig of Lead to the upper end of the village it is a climb of 450ft. The Pig of Lead public house at the foot of the Via Gellia valley closed a few years ago and is now a private house. Little groups of cottages huddled together on odd plots of land along winding streets add to the charm of this attractive, scattered village.

St John's Chapel was erected in 1897 by Sir Guy Dawber of the Arts and Crafts Movement. The building is an architectural gem, with beautiful stained glass windows and many other features. Originally it was built as a private chapel for the residents of Rock House, which stands further down the hillside.

The final stage of the walk provides magnificent views of Matlock.

Looking up the main street at Matlock Bath, a busy little place well stocked with gift shops, cafés and amusements.

Walk Details

Length: 6.25 miles (Short Walk I – 3.5 miles, Short Walk II – 3 miles).

Start/Finish: Matlock Railway (SK297602)/Bus Station (northbound)/car park

Starting Walk: Off the A6 at Matlock, the station is a few yards on the left, beyond the bridge over the Derwent. Cars can be parked in the nearby pay and display car park. The bus station for passengers heading north is by the Railway Station, and for those going south it is on Bakewell Road.

Terrain: Good, surfaced paths all the way to Cromford, with superb views from the fenced viewing points over High Tor*, but with a steep ascent and descent. The return journey is a mixture of woodland paths, quiet roads and field walking; the ascents and descents are not so steep. *****Warning** – Keep to the path and do not walk close to the unprotected cliff edge, and ensure that children and animals are supervised at all times.

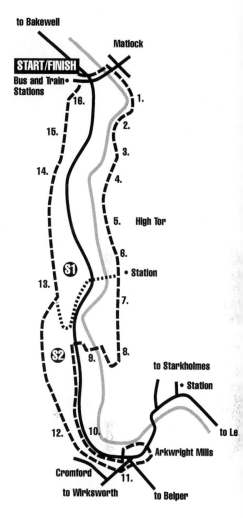

The Route

1. Follow the road to the right out of the bus/rail station to the A6 and turn left over Matlock Bridge. Once over the bridge, go to the right into Hall Leys Park and continue along the path by the river, keeping straight on along an access road to 'Old Matlock' for 50 yards after leaving the park.

2. Go right at a fingerpost sign, cross a footbridge, turn right and follow the river round, with Pic Tor rising steeply above on your left.

3. Pass under a railway bridge and when you arrive at a T-junction of paths, turn left under a bridge and walk up a steep, paved path.

4. As the path flattens out, with houses in front of you, turn sharp right at the sign for the High Tor Grounds and follow a rough track that ascends steadily to the summit. Ensure that you take care to observe the many warning notices about keeping well clear of the cliff edge.

Derwent Pleasure Gardens.

5. At an information board for High Tor Matlock Bath Entrance go to the right and follow the path round, avoiding the path signed for Giddy Edge – it is dangerous in wet weather and for those who do not have a very good head for heights.

6. The path follows an obvious route as it descends steeply down several flights of somewhat uneven steps. At the bottom of the hill, the cable car station is passed and you bear left, close to the railway line for Matlock Bath Railway Station.

7. From the railway station car park walk through the coach park to join a path rising up above the River Derwent. The path climbs steadily, close to the fence to the top of the cliff. Continue along the cliff path as far as you can go, before descending the path on the right.

8. The trail now descends quite steeply along an uneven, stepped path in a zigzag fashion through Hagg Wood. On reaching the river, walk to the right and cross New Bridge.

Looking up towards the Heights of Abraham, where in the summer cable cars glide back and forth.

9. Turn right into Derwent Pleasure Gardens and continue your walk along the riverbank, before going to the left to reach the A6. Turn left along the road and walk down the A6, past Arkwright's, Masson Mill.

10. Shortly after passing the mill, before reaching the road junction, turn left along a concessionary path running between Scarthin Rock and the river. Watch out for a path leading off to the right to the Arkwright Mills complex.

11. Leave Arkwright's Mills and walk up Mill Road, cross the A6 and keep straight on for a short distance. Turn right into Cromford Market Place and follow the road on the right-hand side up Scarthin. After passing Cromford Pond, before the road starts to descend, turn right up a cobbled path signed for Derwent Valley Walk, opposite the former Primitive Methodist Chapel 1853.

Tor Café at Cromford was originally a barber's shop set up by Sir Richard Arkwright.

12. At the end of the cobbles, go to the left through woodland for approximately 150 yards, before turning sharp right at a Derwent Valley Walk waymarker. Continue along a path that doubles back on itself and then winds to the left and straightens out. Where the path forks, keep to the left past a small cave as you begin to climb up the hillside. When you leave the woodland, continue straight on along a rough track at first, then later a tarmac-surfaced lane. Follow the lane as it starts to descend steeply towards Matlock Bath.

13. Approximately 80 yards past the foot entrance to the Heights of Abraham, turn left at a footpath sign for Matlock. The walk continues through woodland, crossing a high footbridge and passing under the cable cars that transport people to and from the Heights of Abraham. At the end of the woodland path, turn right down a farm track.

14. Turn right again, in front of Masson Farm, and walk down the lane. Immediately after passing St John's Church, take the path on the left. Continue along the path, keeping close to the wall, until it divides. Here you bear to the left to walk in a semi-circular direction round a deep depression in the ground.

15. Maintain the same direction, with the wall close on your right, until about 30 yards from the corner of the field. Go through a stile and angle across another field to pass through a gap in the hedge near the top corner.

16. Continue at the same angle to a stile in the wall, and in the next field walk to a marker post at an intersection of paths and turn right towards Matlock. Keep straight on, arriving at Snitterton Road, where you turn right and after only a few yards the A6 is reached, with Matlock Bus and Railway Stations on your left.

Short Walk I

Matlock Walk (3.5 miles)
Route (Matlock {SK297602} – High Tor – Matlock Bath – Heights of Abraham – Matlock)
1. Follow the Matlock to Cromford circular route instructions from Point 1 to Point 6.
2. Leave Matlock Bath Railway Station by the main exit and turn left along the A6.
3. Follow the A6 through Matlock Bath, before going up a steep path by the side of the Fishpond Hotel. At the top, turn right and follow the road round past the Temple Hotel.
4. After passing the hotel, take the first turning on the left to walk up West Bank. At a T-junction, with West Lodge directly in front of you, go to the right. Walk down the road for approximately 80 yards to a footpath sign leading off to the left.
5. Here you rejoin the Matlock to Cromford circular route at Point 13. Follow the instructions to Point 16.

Short Walk II

Matlock Bath Walk (3 miles)
Route (Matlock Bath {SK298586} – Cromford – Scarthin – Matlock Bath)
1. From Matlock Bath Railway Station, follow the instructions for the Matlock to Cromford circular route from Point 7 to Point 12, but taking care not to continue downhill after reaching the foot entrance to The Heights of Abraham.
2. Directly opposite the foot entrance to the Heights of Abraham, turn right and descend a steeply sloping path. At the bottom turn right, past the Temple Hotel, and follow the road round to the left. Just before reaching the A6, turn left down a steep slope leading to South Parade.
3. Go to left, past the Fishpond Hotel, and continue along the pavement through Matlock Bath, crossing the River Derwent by the Station Hotel to walk up to the railway station.

Refreshment Stops
Midland Hotel (Chapter 22/24) is located by the bridge over the Derwent leading to Matlock Bath Railway Station. The wonderfully sited river gardens and terrace are a very popular place with visitors in the summer. (Tel. 01629 582630)

Scarthin Promenade, where the bookshop enjoys a reputation for wide-ranging titles.

West Lodge, the entrance for walkers to the Heights of Abraham.

Wheatcroft's Wharf Café and Wildlife Shop (Chapter 23/24) is situated on Cromford Wharf, on the opposite side of the road from the car park at Cromford Mill. Outside seating is available overlooking the canal. There is also an excellent wholefood restaurant in the Arkwright Mill Complex. (Tel. 01629 823256)

The Boat Inn (Chapter 23/24) dates back to 1872, when Arkwright had it built behind The Greyhound Hotel in Cromford Market Square. The former is for the workers, the latter for visiting businessmen. (Tel. 01629 823282)

Places of Interest in the Locality

Peak District Mining Museum at Matlock Bath is where you get a very realistic impression of what the conditions used to be like for men who toiled underground. After completing your absorbing tour of the museum, you can visit Temple Mine, which has been worked since 1922. The museum is open daily throughout the year. Temple Mine is open on a reduced basis in the winter. (Tel. 01629 583834)

Gulliver's Kingdom at Matlock Bath is a popular theme park for younger children, set in a glorious woodland setting. (Tel. 01925 444888)

The Heights of Abraham at Matlock Bath, where you can take a spectacular journey by cable car to explore two show caverns, follow the woodland trails and enjoy the magnificent view from the Treetops café and restaurant. (Tel. 01629 582365)

Masson Mill at Matlock Bath, where there is a working textile museum and shopping village. It is situated in an internationally famous mill built by Sir Richard Arkwright. Open daily. (Tel. 01629 760208)

Arkwright Mill Complex at Cromford is where the world's first successful water-powered cotton-spinning mill came into production. It is now a world heritage site, and guided tours are available. There is a wholefood restaurant, a number of shops and a large car park. A further restaurant and bookshop has been opened across the road at Cromford Wharf. Open daily. (Cromford Mill Tel. 01629 823256)

A marvellous panoramic view of
Matlock near the end of the walk.

25
Cromford – Sir Richard Arkwright

Cromford is a village of contrasts, with its lower half resting by the gently flowing River Derwent, and the upper half climbing steeply up Cromford Hill to Black Rocks, where there are outstanding views. Majestic as the scenery undoubtedly is, it is not that which attracts visitors from all over the world to Cromford, but the prospect of looking round the area where Sir Richard Arkwright built his cotton mills.

Many new visitors to Cromford though, do not realise that it was the first purpose-built industrial village and that it encompasses the site of the world's first successful water-powered cotton mill. It was from Cromford that its revolutionary methods spread across the rest of the world.

Frequently referred to as the 'Cradle of the Factory System', the importance of Cromford and the Derwent Valley was recognised in 2001, when it was awarded World Heritage Status. The site extends from Masson Mill to the former Derby Silk Mill, a distance of approximately 15 miles, and is the only World Heritage Site in the East Midlands. Cromford has some of the best examples of industrial housing in Britain, standing as an international monument to the Industrial Revolution. It is now protected by a Conservation Order, which encourages the enhancement and repair of these historic buildings.

Arkwright's Cromford Mills, now part of the Derwent Valley World Heritage Site.

Water course at the Arkwright Mill Complex. Water power to run the mills was obtained from Cromford Sough and Bonsall Brook.

The driving force behind the revolution was Richard Arkwright. Having obtained a patent on his spinning frame, he first set up a mill at Nottingham using horse power, but when that proved incapable of development he moved to Cromford. Here he leased a site to the west of Cromford Bridge, close to Smelting Mill Green, where lead ore was smelted. He harnessed the water power of the Bonsall Brook and the Cromford Sough, which was originally constructed to drain lead mines between Wirksworth and Cromford, to drive his machinery.

The first mill was powered by the Cromford Sough until, after obtaining a further patent, a second mill was built in 1776 and came into full production the following year. The new mill, much larger than the first, was powered by two waterwheels, but was destroyed by fire in 1890.

As Arkwright's enterprise expanded, the demand for more water power increased. The

Greyhound Pond, behind the hotel of the same name, was an important part of the system. Together with a series of ponds along the Bonsall Brook, the purpose of its creation as industrial production expanded was purely functional – to ensure a constant head of water for the wheels of the mills to drive the machinery. The brook runs

Visitors on a guided tour of Arkwright's Mills.

The Greyhound Hotel, built in the Market Square by Arkwright.

through the cotton mill site on its way to join the Derwent, upstream from where St Mary's Church now stands.

In 1783–84, several years after setting up business at Cromford, Arkwright built the six-storeyed middle section of Masson Mill, alongside what is now the A6. The chimney and some other buildings on the north side and the newer buildings on the south side were built at a later date by the English Sewing Company. This was his showpiece and it soon became his main factory. It was the only mill to use the River Derwent as a power source, 10 times greater than that at Arkwright's first mill at Cromford. It is now a shopping village on four floors, with a riverside restaurant and a working textile museum.

A major problem that faced Arkwright when he arrived in 1771 was that Cromford was nothing more than a tiny hamlet. The situation became particularly acute in 1776, when the

Looking across The Greyhound Pond to Scarthin.

North Street, where the three storeyed houses are among the finest examples of Industrial Archaeology to be found anywhere.

second mill was built. Arkwright had a flair for business from an early age, however, and was not daunted by the lack of available workers. He set about attracting a workforce by building good-quality houses, with privies, allotments and pigcotes. He paid higher wages than those available for farm work and also supplied working clothes for both sexes and rewarded his overseers with a cow in recognition of particularly good work. Richard Arkwright II built a school and schoolhouse in 1832.

The three-storeyed houses in North Street are among the finest examples of Industrial Archaeology to be found anywhere. Here you can see traces of the long upper windows which provided maximum light for the outworkers at their machines in the attics along both sides of the street. This is where the weavers set up their looms to make the yarn from the mills into fabric. The Arkwright houses on Cromford Hill were built after North Street, some having two and others three storeys. As a testament to its excellent construction, much of the original housing in the village still remains today, for which there is a ready demand.

Arkwright did not stop there and also provided other local amenities and even obtained a charter for a market, held in front of the Greyhound Hotel, where a single-storeyed range of market stalls was built. The markets were held on Saturdays from 1790 onwards for nearly 100 years. In order to encourage trade, prizes were awarded to the traders who had the best stalls and sold the most goods. The Greyhound Hotel was originally known as the Black Dog and has been substantially renovated in recent times. It is surrounded by an interesting collection of shops, including the intriguingly named Mystical Crystals, which is the leading supplier of natural crystals and minerals in the area.

Every September, Arkwright held a festival for the enjoyment of his work people and their families. On the completion of his second mill, in 1776, he held a large party to celebrate. His

The Waterwheel on Water Lane.

workers and their children paraded proudly round the village, led by a large band. After this had finished, they returned to the mill for food and refreshment. The celebrations continued into the evening with a ball.

From the marketplace a narrow one-way road leads to the old mining settlement of Scarthin, where at the bookshop you can reputedly buy a book 24 hours a day and get a cup of coffee and a meal during more normal hours. The café is tucked away behind a secret bookcase door leading to a comfortable, but somewhat curious converted kitchen.

At the end of North Street, a footpath in front of the school takes you down to a stone enclosure, called the Bear Pit. Here you can see the Cromford Sough, which, together with the Bonsall Brook, supplied Arkwright's water power. After passing through the mill, the water crossed the road in an aqueduct to feed the Cromford Canal. Unfortunately, the aqueduct was damaged in a road accident a few years ago, but is currently being restored.

Following Arkwright's death, his son, Richard II, a successful banker and landowner, continued to maintain production but did not expand any further. Cotton spinning gradually left the Derbyshire valleys, and Lancashire became the centre of the industry. A serious water-shortage problem occurred in the mid 1830s with the diversion of the Cromford Sough, which curtailed production and by 1891 production ceased altogether.

The buildings on the mill site were let out for other uses, and during the 1920s most of the site was purchased by a company manufacturing colour pigment for paint, production of which continued until 1979. It was then purchased by the Arkwright Society, who began the immense job of restoring the site, which was heavily contaminated with chemicals and paint.

Open every day of the year except Christmas Day, Cromford Mills are visited by people from all over the world. On 28 September 2010 the Arkwright Society received a very considerable boost with a Lottery grant award of £2 million for the development of the World Heritage Site Gateway facility and a Creative Cluster for businesses in the largest building at Cromford Mill, known as Building 17. The Society expects a significant increase in visitors once the new Gateway facility is complete, which will include an interactive model of the Derwent Valley Mills World Heritage Site. Visitors will be able to gain information on the key locations in the valley, including historical background, what to see and do and how to get there. Plans also include an audiovisual theatre with films about the Derwent Valley and how to make the most of its attractions.

The construction of Cromford Canal was completed in late 1794 to improve the speed of movement of heavy goods in and out of Cromford. Although it was opened after the death of Sir Richard Arkwright, he was a prime mover in the decision to construct the canal. It linked up with the Erewash Canal at Langley Mill, which ran into the River Trent.

Built in two gauges, the canal ran from Langley Mill to the eastern end of the Butterley Tunnel in broad gauge, with 14 locks. From this point, the narrow gauge system took over and there were no locks. The situation was further complicated by the fact that the Butterley Tunnel, 3,000 yards in length, did not have a towpath.

The canal soon became very busy as, apart from the benefits it brought to Arkwright's Cromford Mills, thousands of tons of stone were shipped all over the country from Cromford Wharf. Lead was taken the much shorter distance to the smelter at Lea, using the Nightingale Arm of the canal, a short branch line built by Florence Nightingale's great-uncle. One of the most unusual of shipments was two stone lions, which, having been sculptured at Darley Dale,

The Bear Pit. Here you can see the Cromford Sough, which together with the Bonsall Brook supplied Arkwright's waterpower.

Cromford School and schoolhouse were built by Richard Arkwright II in 1832.

were taken by canal to Liverpool, where they can still be seen standing by the entrance to St George's Hall.

The arrival of the railway era in the mid-1800s gradually took most of the business away from the canal. Then disaster struck at the turn of the 20th century with the collapse of the Butterley Tunnel, which was never rebuilt. The canal continued to be used on both sides, carrying mainly coal and limestone, however, until in 1944 it was finally abandoned as a commercial waterway.

The section of the canal from Cromford to Ambergate has been developed for recreational purposes. The towpath is walkable from Cromford to Ambergate, a distance of just over five miles, and the walk from Cromford Wharf to High Peak Junction is suitable for pushchairs and wheelchairs. It is very rich with wildlife and has been designated a Site of Special Scientific Interest, with the southern end from Ambergate to Whatstandwell being managed as a local nature reserve by Derbyshire Wildlife Trust.

Originally it had been the intention to construct a canal to connect Cromford Canal with the Peak Forest Canal, but difficulties in ensuring an adequate water supply on the moors led to the scheme being dropped. Instead, the Cromford and High Peak Railway was built, which was considered to be an engineering masterpiece and has attracted the interest of railway enthusiasts from all over the world.

The line linked High Peak Junction, at 277ft above sea level, with Whaley Bridge, at 570ft. In the middle it rose to over 1,000ft at Ladmanlow. This involved steep inclines, up and down, which wagons were hauled by steam-driven winding engines. A stretch of the line from High Peak Junction to Dowlow, near Buxton, has been converted into the High Peak Trail for horse riders, cyclists, naturalists and walkers.

Cromford Station, a splendid piece of railway architecture on the Derby to Matlock line, is one of the loveliest railway journeys in the country. It provides a relaxing and scenic way to travel through the southern section of the Derwent Valley, where river, canal, road and rail often run closer together than anywhere else in the country.

The bridge over the Derwent is one of the oldest in England. Alongside are the remains of a bridge chapel and a fishing pavilion. The pavilion is built to the same design as the one in Beresford Dale frequented by Charles Cotton and Izaak Walton. St Mary's Church contains the tomb of Sir Richard Arkwright.

Above the church stands the impressive Willersley Castle, built by Sir Richard, although he died before it was fully completed. It has operated as a hotel since 1927 and is located in 65 acres of grounds, with fine views over the River Derwent. Many of the original features still remain, the most striking of which is the Well Gallery, an oval with a glass dome. It is now a Christian Guilds hotel and conference centre.

Sir Richard Arkwright

Richard Arkwright was born in Preston in 1732, the semi-literate son of a tailor. At an early age he was apprenticed to a barber, and later travelled the country making and selling wigs. It was during this period that he began experimenting with machinery to find a way to spin cotton.

In 1768 Arkwright rented a room in Preston together with John Kay, where they perfected a roller spinning machine, which was initially known as the spinning frame, and later the water frame. The following year he obtained a patent on the machine and moved to Nottingham, where he managed to obtain the finance needed to go into production by taking Jedidiah Strutt and Samuel Need into partnership. As a result, a frame was made to Arkwright's design and production started in 1769 in Nottingham.

At first the frame was driven by horse power, but this proved to be both slow and expensive. Arkwright knew that more power was needed and chose a site at Cromford, where there was a good supply of water that he could utilise to power his proposed factory. Here there was a year-round supply of warm water from Cromford Sough, which was drained from the nearby lead mines at Wirksworth, together with water from Bonsall Brook. As the water from the sough was at a higher temperature than normal, it never froze in winter, which meant that even in the coldest weather the mill never had to stop production.

The construction of the first mill began in August 1771. The yarn was much stronger and more uniform than was possible when spun by hand and could be produced in much larger quantities, and Arkwright's spinning machines soon came to be called water frames. His first mill was of modest in size, but in 1776 he built a second and much larger one. After the second Cromford Mill had been completed, Arkwright's empire began to grow and many more mills were built in Derbyshire, Lancashire, Staffordshire and Scotland.

When Arkwright arrived, Cromford was little more than a tiny hamlet. He had to attract workers and to do this he built most of the village, much as we know it today. With the houses, he built all the facilities that were necessary for village life in those days, even setting up a market. Nor did he forget his past, building a barber's shop, where the popular Tor Café is now situated.

Arkwright was generally regarded as a kindly employer, at a time when many of his contemporaries had no interest in their workers and families. He operated a two-shift system

Cromford Station is a splendid piece of railway architecture, on the Derby to Matlock line.

and had strict rules over timekeeping: the gate to the mill being shut at precisely 6am and 6pm every day and any worker who failed to get through it in time not only lost a day's pay, but was also fined another day's pay. His factories were much cleaner and better maintained than was usual in those days, however. The houses he erected for his employees were well built and described as models of comfort and neatness. As a result of his efforts, he came to be looked upon by the Victorians as the 'the Father of the Factory System'.

The mills that Arkwright built were extensively copied in Great Britain and abroad. Cromford also became a template for other factory villages. It has some of the best examples of industrial housing in Britain, standing as an international monument to the Industrial Revolution. The village is now protected by a conservation order, which encourages the enhancement and repair of the historic buildings.

As a result, Arkwright became very rich and famous, and in 1786 he was knighted. About the same time, work began on building a new home, Willersley Castle, an Adamesque-style mansion, overlooking his Cromford Mills and St Mary's Church, which was originally intended as a private chapel and mausoleum for the Arkwright family. Unfortunately, he died on 3 August 1792, before either had been completed. Both buildings were finished by his son and heir after his death. He is buried at the church, after being interred at Matlock for a short period.

In his lifetime he rose from obscurity to become the first commoner ever to be knighted for his contribution to the cotton-spinning industry. As a result of his achievements, Britain was transformed from an almost self-sufficient country, with an economy based on agriculture and cottage industries, into the workshop of the world.

26
Cromford to Whatstandwell

The Walk

The bridge over the Derwent is one of the oldest in England. Alongside are the remains of a bridge chapel and a fishing pavilion. It is built to the same design as the one in Beresford Dale frequented by Charles Cotton and Izaak Walton. On the opposite side of the road, St Mary's Church contains the tomb of Sir Richard Arkwright.

A visit to the Arkwright complex to discover how Cromford became known as the 'birthplace of the factory system' should not be missed. There are also a number of interesting canal buildings at Cromford Wharf, from where you follow the towpath for 1.25 miles to High Peak Junction. The canal supports an abundance of wildlife, and because of its value as a natural habitat it has been designated a Site of Special Scientific Interest.

Completed in 1794, the Cromford Canal stretched 14.5 miles to Langley Mill, where it joined the Erewash Canal. With a tunnel and two aqueducts, the canal was built to carry limestone from quarries at Crich to the iron foundry at Butterley. It was extended to serve Richard Arkwright's Cromford Mills and it became very busy and profitable as a result.

There was, though, the need to find a much shorter route to link the East Midlands with Manchester. The original intention had been to construct a canal to connect William Jessop's Cromford Canal with Benjamin Outram's Peak Forest Canal. Difficulties in ensuring an adequate water supply on the limestone moors, however, led to the scheme being dropped.

Proposals were then put forward and accepted to build a railway, which was built on a similar alignment to the abandoned canal project. This involved steep inclines, up and down,

Cromford Wharf. The building on the left is now a café and bookshop.

Cromford Wharf. Lifting gear can be seen to the left of the building.

High Peak Junction Workshops date from the earliest days of the railway, being built between 1826 and 1830.

Leawood Pumphouse was built in 1849, following water shortages, to pump water from the river to the canal.

which wagons were hauled up on cables by steam-driven winding engines. Following the closure of the Cromford and High Peak Railway, it was purchased jointly by Derbyshire County Council and the Peak Park Planning Board and, in partnership with the Countryside Commission, converted into the High Peak Trail. At the bottom end of the trail is a catch pit, built following an accident in 1888, in which two wagons jumped across both the canal and the Midland Railway! The last accident occurred in the 1950s.

The High Peak Junction Workshops date from the earliest days of the railway, being built between 1826 and 1830. They remain virtually unchanged since their railway days, with tools, railway artefacts, joiner's bench, forge and bellows. The cast-iron fish-bellied rails on either side of the inspection pit could be the oldest length of railway line in the world still in its original position. A leaflet has been produced to enable visitors to identify the large array of memorabilia on display. At the visitor centre there is a wide selection of books and maps available, as well as an interesting railway video to watch. Light refreshments can be purchased and there are picnic tables outside.

A short distance to the south is Leawood Pumphouse. It was built in 1849, following water shortages, to pump water from the river to the canal. It has been extensively restored by volunteers and is capable of lifting approximately five tons of water each minute, up to a height of 30ft. Open to the public on 'steaming days' during the summer.

Gregory's Tunnel, where an handrail helps guide you through.

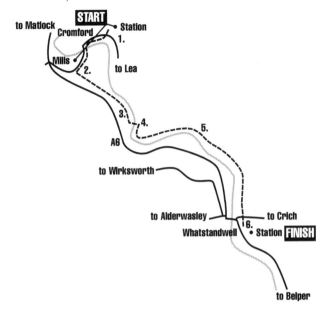

Walk Details

Length: 3 miles.

Start/Finish: Cromford Wharf (SK290571) Cromford Railway Station/Whatstandwell Railway Station.

Starting Walk: Turn off the A6 at Cromford crossroads and head east down Mill Road, where Cromford Wharf is on the right by a pay and display car park. Rail users should turn right at the station entrance and follow the road round to reach the wharf. Buses stop at Cromford crossroads on the A6 (northbound 50 yards before crossroads are reached, southbound close to the traffic lights).

Finishing Walk: A regular train service is available from Whatstandwell and buses run from stops on either side of the A6 close to the Derwent Hotel, next to the bridge over the Derwent. To continue the walk, go to the Whatstandwell to Ambergate route section.

Cromford Canal is designated an Area of Special Scientific Interest.

Following the Cromford Canal towpath, from the Wharf to High Peak Junction, is a pleasant one and a quarter mile walk.

Terrain: An easy walk along the towpath of the Cromford Canal. The towpath can get quite muddy after heavy rainfall. Rail users have a short walk along the pavement from the railway station to Cromford Wharf.

The Route

1. From Cromford Wharf continue forward beyond the wharf buildings, keeping to the left of the canal to walk along the towpath of the Cromford Canal for approximately 1.25 miles to reach High Peak Junction.

2. Shortly after passing Leawood Pumphouse, when you see the footpath sign for Lea, cross the bridge over the canal to walk along the right-hand towpath.

3. Soon Gregory's Tunnel is reached, where a handrail helps guide you through the tunnel. Robin Hood, a tiny hamlet on the left-hand side of the canal, is passed before Whatstandwell is reached.

4. Continue alongside the towpath, where the road over the canal leads up from Whatstandwell to Crich. After 100 yards go to the right over a footbridge, which leads to Whatstandwell Station.

House by the riverbank at the tiny hamlet of Robin Hood, which is not even shown on the Ordnance Survey Map.

27
Whatstandwell to Ambergate

The Walk

Whatstandwell is located in a most picturesque and thickly wooded section of the Derwent Valley, but the traveller on the busy A6 only catches a brief glimpse of the village, probably seeing little more than the entrance to the railway station, the hotel and the bridge over the River Derwent. Passengers on the train will almost certainly see even less, as part of the route goes through a tunnel, running under a house and the bankside.

In the past there have been several attempts to trace the origin of the name 'Whatstandwell', but most people now seem to agree that it was named after Walter Stonewall. At the time when the bridge was built in 1391, Walter, or Wat, Stonewall rented a cottage where the bridge was constructed, which was mentioned in the agreement with the landowner. Prior to the building of the bridge, a ford crossed the river at that point.

According to historical notes published in 1956, it was said that 'Whatstandwell has no legal nor administrative existence. It was never a lordship or a manor, neither is it a civil or ecclesiastical parish.' Officially it is part of Crich Carr, but the Midland Railway named their station Whatstandwell and the Ordnance Survey honoured the name. Local people also used the name and gradually, with the passage of time and slight modifications, it became accepted. The

The Derwent Arms at Whatstandwell, where there has been an inn for over 300 years.

Whatstandwell is believed to have been named after Walter Stonewall, who rented a cottage by the bridge.

village now extends well beyond the river bridge, its little grey-stone cottages merging quietly into the background of wood and cliff along the roadside.

The Crich to Holloway road leads up the hill from the bridge, and is the road that Florence Nightingale used on her two-mile journey to her home at Lea Hurst after she returned from the Crimea. Florence wanted no fuss, despite having become a legend in her own lifetime for her services to the nursing profession. Nor did she ever forget her Derbyshire roots and her native village, providing many of the books held in the village coffee and reading rooms, where there was also a billiard room. Members paid sixpence per quarter towards the reading room and nine pence per quarter for billiards.

Despite the fact that Whatstandwell is so far from the sea, it is the place where Ellen MacArthur, the celebrated yachtswoman, grew up. She shot to fame after finishing second in the gruelling Vendée Globe single-handed round-the-world yacht race. Then, in early 2005, Ellen completed her bid to break the record for the fastest person to sail single-handedly around the world, beating the previous record set by Frenchman Francis Joyon. Thanks to her single-handed record-breaking exploits, she was the youngest person ever to be made a Dame.

The construction of the Cromford Canal was completed in late 1794 to improve the movement of heavy goods in and out of Cromford. It linked up with the Erewash Canal at Langley Mill, which ran into the River Trent. This provided a connection with Derby and Nottingham, and beyond that with Liverpool and Manchester by the Trent and Mersey Canal. In the mid-1800s the railway era arrived and gradually took most of the business away from the canal.

It is claimed that nowhere in England do the four methods of transport, road, rail, river and canal, run as closely together as they do here. Although the canal is now only used for leisure

The Stationmaster's House at Whatstandwell next to the A6.

purposes, the railway line is one of the most scenically attractive in the country, but now runs no further than Matlock.

The walk along the Cromford Canal towpath takes you through a nature reserve, where you can watch the waterfowl busily looking for tasty morsels of food and keep a sharp eye out for other wildlife. You next reach Ambergate, a product of the 19th century, which in its heyday was one of the most important railway junctions in the Midlands, with nearly 50 staff employed and handling 240 trains a day. Now a single platform serves the Derby–Matlock line.

The railway tunnels under a house and the bankside at Whatstandwell.

Walk Details

Length: 2 miles.

Start/Finish: Whatstandwell Railway Station (SK332541) – Ambergate Railway Station.

Starting Walk: The railway station is on the right side of the A6 when travelling north from Belper to Matlock, a short distance before the B5035 turn-off for Crich. A car park is available for rail users at the station. There is also room for a small number of cars to park by the western side of the canal on the B5035 Crich road, where you join the canal towpath and walk south. Bus stops are on either side of the A6, close to Derwent Hotel and the bridge over the river.

Finishing Walk: A regular train service is available from Ambergate

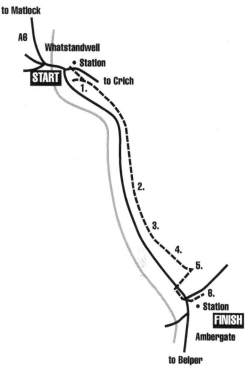

Branches overhanging the canal near Ambergate, where it becomes more overgrown.

It is claimed that nowhere in England do the four methods of transport, road, rail, river and canal, run as closely together.

and buses run from stops on either side of the A6, close to the Hurt Hotel on the southern side of the road intersection. To continue the walk, go to the Ambergate to Belper route section.

Terrain: Easy walking, mostly along the towpath of the Cromford Canal. It can be muddy in wet weather.

The Route

1. Leave Whatstandwell Station by the footbridge over the railway track, climbing halfway up a flight of steps to reach the canal bank. Non-rail users should access the canal from the Whatstandwell to Crich road and head south.

Good views open up on the walk.

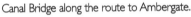

Canal Bridge along the route to Ambergate.

Near Ambergate houses start to appear, before Chase Road is reached.

2. Turn right along the towpath of the Cromford Canal, where the canal, road, rail and river almost converge. After about a mile you pass under a bridge, which carries a footpath leading to Crich and Crich Carr.

3. Shortly after passing a stone-built cottage, go under another bridge and continue along the canal towpath.

4. The views to the west are now more open, and soon after passing a brick-built cottage you will notice a further bridge in front of you. Do not go under the bridge, but go up the path by its side, where a sign marked 'Cromford 5 miles' points back in the direction you have walked.

5. Turn right down Chase Road, going under a railway bridge, to reach the bottom of the road. Go to the left along the A6 (bus stops are further along the road, past the Hurt Arms) and turn left along the A610, opposite the Hurt Arms Hotel.

6. After going under the railway bridge, turn right up Station Approach to reach Ambergate Station.

Railway Bridge on Chase Road, with houses along side the A6 in the background.

28
Cromford to Ambergate Circular Walk

The Walk

After leaving Cromford and the High Peak Trail behind, excellent views of the Derwent Valley are soon enjoyed and the scattered village of Alderwasley is reached. The church stands in the grounds of Alderwasley Hall, and few churches in England can be in such a delightful setting. A cedar tree stands guard, while just below a sparkling stream runs, with little waterfalls and ornamental lakes. The hall was once the home of the Hurt family, who acquired considerable wealth from lead mining, and later smelting.

Shining Cliff Woods is a Site of Special Scientific Interest due to the large variety

Mill Road at Cromford is also known as Mill Lane.

All Saints Church at Alderwasley stands in the grounds of Alderwasley Hall.

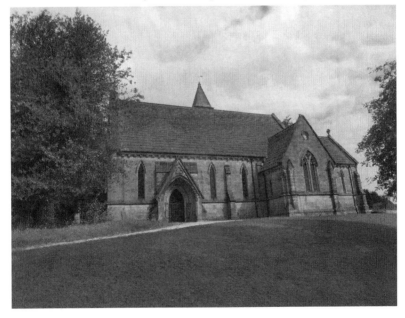

All Saints Church Alderwasley – church entrance.

Alderwasley Hall, seen in the distance, was once the home of the Hurt family.

of plants and animals found in this ancient woodland. It was also the home of Betty Kenny and her husband, who came every year with their young family to burn charcoal. They lived in an improvised hut by a huge yew tree said to be 2,000 years old. According to legend, a bough of the tree was hollowed out to form a cradle for their children – the probable origin of the nursery rhyme *Rock-a-bye-baby*.

At the side of St Anne's Church, Holly Lane leads down to Halfpenny Bridge, which crosses the River Derwent. As the name suggests, anyone crossing was required to pay halfpence at the toll house. This has been demolished, but the Turnpike Gateposts, near to the Ambergate Chippy, remain as a reminder of that era.

Ambergate's first railway station was built by the North Midland Railway, one of the three companies that four years later, in 1844, formed the Midland Railway. Further developments took place as business expanded. A southern curve was added in 1863, followed 13 years later by a middle curve, creating an unusual triangular junction with the platforms set around the triangle. In its heyday Ambergate was one of the most important railway junctions in the Midlands, with nearly 50 staff employed and handling 240 trains a day. Now a single platform serves the Derby-Matlock line.

Peter Nightingale II, who was born in 1736 and known as 'Mad Peter' because of his reckless horse riding, gambling and heavy drinking, took over the family business at Lea. His lifestyle did not seem to affect his entrepreneurial capabilities, and he established a successful lead-smelting business at Lea Bridge and extended an arm of the Cromford Canal up to where Smedley's car park stands today. Florence Nightingale – renowned throughout the world for her nursing skills – was a direct descendant.

It seems hard to believe, but High Peak Junction was once the starting point for a railway line over the

Alderwasley War Memorial is situated in a field looking towards Alderwasley School.

Looking over the Derwent Valley towards Crich Stand.

moors. It linked High Peak Junction, at 277ft above sea level, with Whaley Bridge, at 517ft. In the middle it rose to over 1,000ft at Ladmanlow. Stretching for 33 miles in length, the line was fully opened in 1831, when it was used to transport minerals, corn, coal and other commodities from one canal to the other. It has now been converted into a trail.

High Peak Trail leads up to Black Rocks, which have been a tourist destination for centuries, as graffiti chiselled into the rock testifies. The coming of the railways to Matlock and Wirksworth made it easier for people to visit the rocks; some came to explore and admire the wonderful views, others to engage in the more strenuous activity of climbing the rocks.

The small town of Wirksworth, which stands virtually at the centre of Derbyshire, about two miles to the south of the Peak District National Park boundary, was the centre of the English lead-mining industry when it was at its height. Lead mining in the area goes back to at least Roman times. The Barmote Court at Wirksworth was set up in 1288 to enforce lead-mining laws, which even at that time were of great antiquity. It is almost certainly the oldest industrial court in Britain, and possibly in the world; it still sits twice a year at Moot Hall in Chapel Lane.

Between 1600 and 1780 lead mining reached a peak, before finally declining during the latter part of the 19th century. When miners were forced

Stone seat by the track approaching Shining Cliff Woods.

deeper and deeper for the ore, flooding problems became even more severe and made extraction uneconomic. The discovery of rich deposits of easily accessible lead ore at Broken Hill in Australia forced prices down even further, resulting in the closure of many mines.

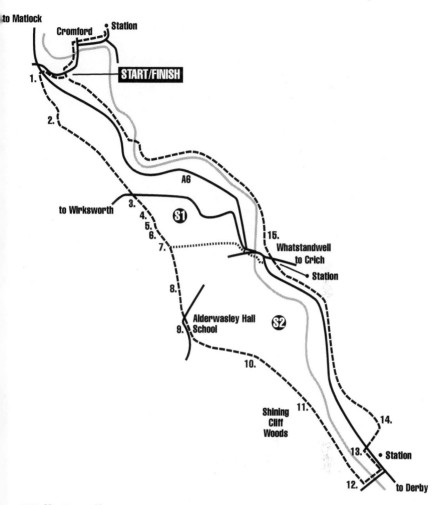

Walk Details

Length: 10.25 miles (Short Walk I – 6.5 miles, Short Walk II – 4.5 miles).

Start/Finish: Cromford Wharf (SK290571).

Starting/Finishing the Walk: Turn off the A6 at Cromford crossroads and head east down Mill Road. Cromford Wharf is opposite to the car park entrance at the Arkwright Mill Complex. The railway station is over the bridge across the River Derwent on the Lea and Holloway road. There is a pay and display car park at Cromford Wharf, off Mill Road. Buses stop at Cromford crossroads on the A6 (northbound 50 yards before the cross roads are reached, southbound close to the traffic lights). The railway station is a short distance further east.

Alderwasley where the path divides to the south-west of the school.

Terrain: A steady walk up from Cromford to the High Peak Trail is followed by a comparatively easy undulating walk along easy-to-follow paths to Alderwasley, with some outstanding views along the way. Shining Cliff Woods are delightful, particularly in the spring when the woods are carpeted with bluebells. The section of the walk along the Cromford Canal provides for easy walking and an opportunity to enjoy the abundance of wildlife it has to offer. The towpath can be very muddy in places after prolonged heavy rainfall

The Route

1. Walk up Mill Road from Cromford Wharf to the A6, going over the road at the pelican crossing and turning left towards Belper and then right into Intake Lane. After passing a number of houses, the surface of the lane changes from tarmac to an uneven track and passes through a tunnel underneath the High Peak Trail.

2. Continue along the track for a short distance, then go to the right where the track divides and walk along the edge of the wood. Go through a stile and turn left down Intake Lane. Continue along the lane without deviating to reach Longway Lane.

3. Cross the lane and go through the stile on the opposite side into a field. Walk up the slope, heading slightly to the left to a stile at the top of the field. After going over the stile, follow an enclosed path uphill into a wood, where you continue in the same direction along an obvious track.

4. When the track reaches the top of the hill, the route soon takes you to the right, along the edge of the wood. The wood is departed by a stile into a field, where you keep close to the wall on the left to pass Watfield Farm and buildings.

5. Go through the stile by the farm gate and continue ahead for 200 yards down a lane, passing Yew Tree Cottage. Turn right by three waymark indicators and cross a stile. Walk diagonally down the field to a stile that leads you along an enclosed path past Watergate Farm.

6. Cross the farm drive and a tiny field on the right to go over a stile and walk diagonally up the next field. After going over the stile at the top of the field, keep close to the field boundary in the next field to arrive at the corner of the field.

7. Here you have an intersection of paths with a gate and stile. Go over the stile. As soon as you are over the stile, turn sharp left to go over another stile. Follow the field boundary as it gently descends, until near the bottom you bear slightly to the right to cross a stile.

8. Continue in the same direction down the next field, with the hedge on your right, before turning right to go through a stile near the bottom corner of the field. Follow the field boundary on your left as you proceed across the field, before the path turns sharply to the left by an area of woodland. Walk straight down the last field, keeping close to the fence on your right, to reach New Road.

9. Turn right along the road and follow it round to the left, down Higg Lane past Alderwasley Hall School, bearing to the left over a stile by a gate where the road starts to rise. Go forward a short distance, turning left by the corner of the school playing field into a large field. Angle to the right across the field to a marker post you can see in the distance.

10. Continue to maintain the same direction after passing the waymarker, shortly leaving the field by a stile. Follow a wide bracken-clad path down through Alderwasley Park, eventually arriving at a stile that takes you into Shining Cliff Woods.

11. Keep straight ahead without deviating as you follow a rough track down through the woods. On reaching a T-junction of tracks, go to the right along a wide track, at first through woodland and then along an access road to mainly derelict factory buildings.

12. After passing the last building, the path again goes through woodland before reaching a Y-junction, where you go to the left along an authorised vehicular access track, at the end of which you arrive at a minor road. Here you turn left towards Ambergate, crossing Halfpenny Bridge and walking up past St Anne's Church to the A6, where you turn left.

13. Follow the A6 past the Hurt Arms and several houses on the opposite side of the road, before turning to the right up Chase Road, passing under a railway bridge and shortly afterwards going to the left to join the towpath of the Cromford Canal.

14. At this point you will notice a sign by the canal bank indicating 'Cromford 5 miles'. Continue along the towpath, soon passing under a bridge, which carries a footpath leading to Crich and Crich Carr. As you reach Whatstandwell, the railway station can soon be seen on the left-hand side of the canal, where the canal, river, road and railway almost converge.

15. Follow the towpath under the bridge carrying the road over the

Shining Cliff Woods is a Site of Special Scientific Interest due to the large variety of plants and animals found in the area.

Corner Café at Ambergate.

canal up from Whatstandwell to Crich, past the picturesque hamlet of Robin Hood on the opposite side of the canal. Shortly afterwards Gregory's Tunnel is reached, where a handrail helps to guide you through the tunnel. After passing Leawood Pumphouse you arrive at High Peak Junction, before continuing on your way along the canal back to Cromford Wharf.

Short Walk I

Cromford Walk (6.5 miles)
Route (From Cromford {SK290571} – High Peak Trail – Intake Lane – Whatstandwell – High Peak Junction – Cromford)

1. Follow the Cromford to Ambergate circular route instructions from Point 1 to Point 6. Do not go over the stile, but turn to face the Derwent Valley and head directly down a series of fields, keeping close to the field boundary on the right. Crich Stand, which can be seen in the distance on the other side of the valley, acts as a guide.

2. After passing the rear of Hankin Farm, follow the path to the right of a cottage and walk down the side of the drive, along the waymarked path. Where the drive bends to the right, continue along the path in front of you through an area of woodland. At the bottom of which turn right and walk to a minor road.

3. Cross the road, go over a stile into a small field, walk down to the A6 and go over the bridge across the River Derwent. Continue straight ahead and walk up the road towards Crich and turn left onto the Cromford Canal towpath.

4. Follow the canal along, passing High Peak Junction, to reach Cromford Wharf.

Short Walk II

Ambergate Walk (4.5 miles)
Route (From Ambergate {SK349516} – Whatstandwell – Alderwasley – Shining Cliff Woods – Ambergate)

1. From the Hurt Arms on the A6 at Ambergate, follow the Cromford to Ambergate circular route instructions from Point 13 to Point 14.

2. At Whatstandwell, leave the canal towpath by the Whatstandwell to Crich road, walk down to the A6 and cross the bridge over the River Derwent.

3. Once over the bridge, go over a stile in front of you, walk through a small field and cross a minor road that leads up to Alderwasley. Follow the rough track opposite, before going to the left along a path through an area of woodland. At the end of which you walk up a waymarked path to the left of a driveway to pass by the side of a cottage to a stile at the rear.

4. The path continues to climb up past Hankin Farm through a series of fields, keeping close to the wall on the left. As the path dips, keep straight on to reach a stile by a gateway at an intersection of paths. Here you rejoin the Cromford to Ambergate circular route at Point 7; follow the instructions to Ambergate at Point 12.

Refreshment Stops

Derwent Hotel (Chapter 26/28) at Whatstandwell was formerly called the Bull's Head. There has been an inn here for over 300 years. There is outside seating at the rear. (Tel. 01773 856616)

Hurt Arms Hotel (Chapter 27/28) was built in 1874 and named after the Hurts, former Lords of the Manor, who lived at Alderwasley Hall. Extensive beer garden and children's play area. (Tel. 01773 852006)

Corner Café (Chapter 27/28) at Ambergate is rightly very popular, but is limited to Saturday, Sunday and Bank Holiday, opening normally from 8am–2pm. (Tel. 01773 856605)

Places of Interest in the Locality

High Peak Junction is at the start of the High Peak Trail. Light refreshments are available during peak season. Picnic tables are pleasantly sited overlooking the Cromford Canal. (Tel. 01629 822831)

Middleton Top Visitor Centre is further along the High Peak Trail. It tells the story of the Cromford and High Peak Railway and provides information, maps, walk leaflets, books, gifts and refreshments. There is a car park, toilets, cycle hire centre, engine house (telephone for details of opening days) and picnic site. Normally open daily from Easter to beginning of September. Weekends only during the winter. (Tel. 01629 823204)

Steeple Grange Light Railway is located close to Black Rocks on the High Peak Trail. It is an 18-inch gauge line built on the trackbed of the CHPR, now the High Peak Trail. Scenic rides of approximately 20 minutes are provided in an area of Special Scientific Interest. Special events are held regularly, please telephone for precise details. (Tel. 01246 235497)

The National Stone Centre is located off the High Peak Trail at Wirksworth. It tells the story of stone, its geological and industrial history. The exhibition shows how advanced technology makes use of stone in an incredible number of ways. Outside the visitor centre, the quarry trail takes you back over 300 million years. Open all year, seven days a week. (Tel. 01629 824833)

Lea Gardens is a short distance from High Peak Junction, where a rare collection of rhododendrons, azaleas, alpines and conifers are to be found in a lovely woodland setting. You can sit inside the attractive teashop, or outside when the weather is suitable. Plants can be purchased. (Tel. 01629 534380)

Crich Tramway Village boasts a large array of vintage trams from all over the world. Unlimited rides through a period street to stunning views over the Derwent Valley. (Tel. 01773 854321)

Lea Mills Factory Shop, the home of John Smedley Ltd, who are well known for the high quality of their garments and rich manufacturing heritage (Tel. 01629 530426)

29
Belper and Milford – Jedidiah Strutt

Arriving in Belper as most do, along the overcrowded A6 road, the main desire is to reach the other side as quickly as possible. But for those who take the time to explore, a completely different picture emerges – of a small town so rich in industrial heritage that it is not only of

national importance, but occupies a pre-eminent position on the world stage.

Belper is now universally recognised as part of the 'birthplace of the factory system'. Further recognition came in 2001, when the 15-mile section of the Derwent Valley from Masson Mill to the former Derby Silk Mill was awarded World Heritage Status.

The story of Belper really begins as a small settlement in the royal hunting forest of Duffield Frith, when it was given the name of 'Beaurepaire', which means 'beautiful place'. In the mid 1200s a small stone church was built in a clearing so that the foresters and their

Entrance to Strutt's North Mill Visitor Centre at Belper.

The 'Gangway' across the Belper to Ashbourne road. Gun embrasures can be seen in the wall.

The Horseshoe Weir was regarded in the late 18th century as one of the outstanding engineering structures in the country.

families would have somewhere to worship. It was first dedicated to Thomas Becket, but rededicated to St John during the Reformation. Today, it has changed very little in appearance, but is now used for the joint purpose of Town Council Chambers and Heritage Centre.

The making of nails was Belper's first main industry. Hunting was a regular pastime in the area and huntsmen used to bring their horses to Belper to be shod. The horse nails made in Belper were considered the best in the country and attracted hunting men from miles around. The nearby iron and coal industries fuelled the production of the nails, and it would also seem that the qualities of the two minerals gave the finished articles that extra bit of superiority.

The earliest written record of nail making in Belper goes back to 1260, but it is likely that nails were made there shortly after the Norman Conquest as the de Ferrers family, who were principal iron masters for

Belper River Gardens with its flowerbeds, arboretum, bandstand, water gardens, children's playground and boating facilities.

181

Nailers Cottage in Joseph Street. The making of nails was Belper's first main industry.

William the Conqueror, had introduced iron forges to the area.

Originally the nailer worked for himself with the help of his family. The children would carry the coal, his wife would work the bellows and he would fashion the nails. It was a hard life, the work hot and exhausting. Perhaps as a result of the hot, exhausting work, the nailers had a reputation as hard drinkers and often got into fights; many were imprisoned for drunkenness and disorderly behaviour. As a rule they did not work on St Mondays, which they kept as a day for celebrations, or recovery! Frequently this extended to St Tuesday and sometimes to St Wednesday as well. In the 1800s the trend changed and larger businesses were set up, but wages were poor and strikes not uncommon. Competition from machinery sent the industry into decline and, from a high of 1,400 men and women, the number of workers dropped to 38 in 1901. Nail making is no more in Belper, but the local football team's nickname is 'The Nailers' and a nailer's workshop still remains.

The gaps in Long Row are where houses have been demolished to make way for George Stephenson's railway.

The War Memorial Garden in Belper.

Up until 1770 Belper was only a small village surrounded by fields, with a population of just over 500 people. Around this time Richard Arkwright went into partnership with Samuel Need of Nottingham and Jedidiah Strutt to develop a water-powered mill at Cromford. A few years later Belper and then Milford were transformed, with mills springing up along the Derwent, and houses and other service requirements being built by Jedidiah to meet the demands of the rapidly increasing population.

Rarely can one man and his family have created such a lasting impact on the economy of a small town as the Strutts did on Belper. Jedidiah Strutt was born on a small farm at Blackwell, near Alfreton. From a young age he had an obsessive interest in machinery, but when his uncle died and left him a smallholding he took it over and married Elizabeth Woollatt, whom he had met when in apprenticeship as a wheelwright. His brother-in-law, who worked for a hosiery firm in Derby, knowing of Jedidiah's interest in machinery, told him of the problems they were having in trying to adapt their machines to make stockings in a ribbed pattern to stop them from falling down the leg; everything they had tried had failed. Immediately Jedidiah set about the task of finding a solution.

He spent many hours in his attic experimenting, neglecting his farmwork in the process. At last he succeeded and the closer-fitting stockings that resulted were a great success. He went into partnership with his brother-in-law, opening a stocking factory in Derby, and patented his 'Derby Rib Machine'. Wishing to expand his business further, he went into partnership with Samuel Need, and their quest for better cotton thread for their hosiery resulted in Richard Arkwright being invited to join them.

Using the power of the River Derwent to drive the machinery, Jedidiah built his first cotton mill, the South Mill, at Belper in 1776. This was followed about 10 years later by the first North

St. John's Chapel Heritage Centre contains an interesting collection of old photographs of Belper and memorabilia.

Mill, destroyed by fire in 1803. A compassionate man, he had strong religious beliefs and showed great concern for the welfare of his employees. He provided them with houses, education and religious training. Row upon row of good-quality houses were built. Almost a century later, three of the streets were named after Jedidiah's sons, William, George and Joseph.

A strict disciplinarian, his employees were fined heavily for lateness or bad behaviour, and he insisted on them going to a place of worship on Sundays and the children attending school regularly. Model farms were established at Belper and Milford, where food was produced so employees could be supplied at reasonable cost, with credit facilities available. Jedidiah ended his days at Exeter House in Derby in 1797 and was buried at the Unitarian Chapel in Belper that he had built.

Jedidiah left three very able sons, under whose control the cotton mills at Belper grew to become the largest in the country. William, his eldest son, was a pioneer in making buildings fireproof, and he rebuilt the North Mill in 1803, which was considered a masterpiece of engineering technology. The brick arch floors are supported on an iron frame and contribute to making the mill fireproof. The mill has its own ingenious warm-air heating system and a hoist between floors.

George's grandson, Herbert Strutt, founded the school that bears his name. Joseph was mayor of Derby in 1835 and gave the Arboretum to the people of Derby as a public park. Modern Belper is largely a product of the Strutts, under whose influence the population rose from just over 500 to 10,000 in 50 years. All around the town are signs of their benevolence.

One of Jedidiah's apprentices, by the name of Samuel Slater, gained fame and notoriety when, after learning all he could in Belper, he set off for America in 1789. He knew that many unsuccessful attempts had been made there to set up machinery to manufacture cotton goods. He carried all the information in his head, as persons leaving British ports were carefully searched for plans to prevent industrial espionage.

On arriving in America he used his expertise to put the American cotton industry on its feet. He became a very rich man, having benefited from personal training by Jedidiah, but repaid him by stealing his secrets and using them to set up mass production in the American cotton industry.

On either side of the gangway, over the Ashbourne road, which connected the mills, are small gun embrasures, put there to ward off Luddites, but fortunately never used. North Mill is now the home of the Strutt's North Mill Visitor Centre, where regular guided tours are arranged of this fascinating mill, with its absorbing displays of hand spinning wheels, Hargreaves's Spinning Jenny and many more exhibits that bring this old mill back to life.

It is now possible to walk from the impressive and extremely interesting visitor centre, past the semi-circular weir into the River Gardens with its flowerbeds, arboretum, bandstand, water gardens, children's playground and boating facilities. East Mill, which stands by the side of North Mill, is a seven-storey red-brick building of 1912, where surprisingly the bricks were laid from the inside without the use of scaffolding. It was formerly occupied by the English Sewing Company, but is now put to other uses.

The first industrial housing in Belper was built in Short Row and the next in Long Row. The gaps in Long Row are where houses have been demolished to make way for George Stephenson's railway, which runs through the middle of the town under no less than 10 bridges.

Larger houses were provided in blocks of four for mill overseers in the Clusters, and just round the corner in Joseph Street is an old nailer's workshop. St Peters Church, off Church Lane, was built to meet the spiritual needs of a growing population when St John's Chapel became too small to satisfy the growing demand.

Near the chapel is an area known as The Butts, where archery practice once took place and where horse fairs were held twice a year. The marketplace was at one time an area of wasteland where in 1762 John Wesley preached. This leads down to King Street, the main shopping area.

Along Derby Road is the imposing Herbert Strutt School, built when a report indicated that the town needed a school of good standard for children of 11 years and over. This provided the impetus for George Herbert Strutt to provide the land and build the school. Across the road is the equally imposing Babington House. Originally built as a workhouse, it was upgraded to an A1 Hospital following the Poor Law changes of 1930.

Hosiery and knitwear were major industries in Belper in the late 18th century. The industry was organised on the 'putting out system', where a master hosier put out yarn to framework knitters who worked from their homes. The work was spread between villages within a 25 mile radius of Belper in order to prevent knitters joining forces in unions to force the price up. The week following the distribution of the yarn, the stockings would be collected and the knitters paid for their work.

During this period, John Ward established his spinning business in Belper and bought cotton from the Strutts. In the early 19th century George Brettle joined the business and the firm started to expand rapidly. By 1812 the company was employing over 1,000 staff and even had a London address. Seventeen years later they were the leading hosiers in the country, with 4,000 framework knitting machines under their control.

Following William Ward's death in 1833, George Brettle renamed the business George Brettle & Co., building a new warehouse on the site, occupied since 1994 by the De Bradelei

Mill Shop. By 1844 Brettle's was employing over 6,000 frames. In addition to stockings, panteloons, drawers, gloves and caps were also manufactured. Outwork ceased in the 1930s.

Belper's reputation for the manufacture of hosiery and other cotton goods was known throughout the country, and stockings were supplied for George III and his granddaughter Queen Victoria. It is also believed that the cotton vest worn by Lord Nelson at the Battle of Trafalgar was made in the town.

In 1936 the company employed 1,500 people in Belper and 500 in London, with 60 representatives. In 1964, however, it was taken over by Courtaulds and closed 23 years later. The premises now help to bring visitors into the town for the retail shopping experience.

The former mills and most of the ancillary buildings at Milford have been destroyed.

Jedidiah Strutt

Jedidiah Strutt was born in South Normanton in 1926 into a farming family and part of a small Presbyterian community with strong Nonconformist religious views. His father soon realised that Jedidiah was not interested in his schoolwork or helping his elder brother on the farm. He was obsessed with experimenting with machinery, so at the age of 14 he was sent as an apprentice to a wheelwright in Findern. His father found him lodgings in the village with the Woollatt family. The village was also the home of one of the largest Nonconformist Academies in the country and came under the influence of Ebenezar Latham, a doctor, teacher and minister, who was associated with the Woollatt family.

After serving as an apprentice for seven years, he moved from one job to another in the Leicester area. Jedidiah returned to Blackwell, a village adjoining South Normanton, when his uncle died and left him a smallholding. At the age of 28 he wrote to Elizabeth Woollatt, with whom he had grown up in Findern, and asked her to marry him. She accepted and they settled down on the farm, but he still yearned to be involved with machinery.

The opportunity to get involved with machines again came when Elizabeth's brother, who worked for a hosiery firm in Derby, contacted him. He explained the difficulties they were having designing a machine to make ribbed stockings to stop them from slipping down the leg. Immediately Jedidiah set to work to find a solution. After several attempts he succeeded and invented the 'Derby Rib Machine'.

The stockings became very popular and Jedidiah and his family moved to Derby in 1758, where he went into partnership with his brother-in-law. They faced many difficulties, but eventually received a patent and began production with financial backing from Samuel Need, a

The King William IV at Milford looks out across the bridge over the Derwent.

wealthy Nottingham hosier. The business became very successful, but production was mainly limited to raw silk hose for the specialised London market. Interest in silk eventually started to decline in favour of cotton.

At about this time Richard Arkwright moved from Lancashire to Nottingham in search of financial support for his new invention for spinning cotton. He received backing from Jedidiah and Samuel Need, and it is thought that Strutt's suggestions for improvements enabled Arkwright to put the water frame into full production. The partnership was dissolved at the time of Need's death in 1776.

Arkwright's Mill at Cromford used water power to drive the machinery and was soon successful and he continued to expand his operations at Cromford, and eventually at other locations. This led Jedidiah to build his first cotton mill at Belper in 1776, which was followed by the building of further mills at both Belper and Milford.

Apart from the cotton mills that soon dominated Belper and Milford, row after row of houses appeared, as did other amenities. Jedidiah expected his millworkers to work hard, but in return he was a generous employer and benefactor. He was also a devoted father to his five children. Unfortunately, his wife died when the youngest child, Joseph, was only eight years old.

After living at Milford House near his mills for a time, he remarried in the early 1780s and shortly afterwards moved to Exeter House in Derby, where he died in 1797. He was buried in a vault under the Unitarian Chapel that he had built at Belper, leaving behind three very able sons, under whose control the cotton mills at Belper grew to become the largest in the country.

30
Ambergate to Belper

The Walk

At the side of St Anne's Church, Holly Lane leads down to Halfpenny Bridge, which crosses the River Derwent. As the name suggests, anyone crossing was required to pay one halfpenny at the tollhouse. The tollhouse has been demolished, but the Turnpike Gateposts, near to the Ambergate Chippy, remain as a reminder of that era.

Close to the bridge, the River Amber flows into the Derwent. To the north Kate Kenyon had her home in Shining Cliff Woods, together with her husband, Luke, and their eight children. The Yew tree under which they sheltered is known as Betty Kenny's Tree, famed for its association with the nursery rhyme *Rock-a-bye-baby*. The babies were rocked to sleep in its branches.

There are excellent views of Crich Stand as you descend the path past Dairywood Farm. Built in 1923, it is dedicated to the memory of the men who died in the Sherwood Foresters

Whitewells Lane is a quiet country lane with magnificent views of the Derwent Valley.

The Hurt Arms, Ambergate, was built in 1874 and named after the former Lords of the Manor, the Hurts, who lived at Alderwasley.

The path to Wyver Farm, with Coppice Wood in the distance.

Regiment during World War One. Subsequently, the men who served in World War Two have also been remembered. It is a landmark that can be seen for miles around and on a bright day it is possible to see Lincoln Cathedral, 50 miles away. It is thought that a bonfire was lit at Crich Stand to celebrate the defeat of the Spanish Armada; now a light powered by electricity lights up the sky.

On Wyver Lane the reed-fringed Wyver Lane Pool, a nature reserve, is owned by Derbyshire Wildlife Trust. It is one of the few remaining areas of wet grassland in the mid-Derwent. The reserve has many resident bird species, including Canada geese, tufted duck and little grebe. Numerous other species visit during the year, including wildfowl that have flown south to avoid exposure to extreme winter cold. There is a bird hide, but the site is kept locked

Wyver Pool is a nature reserve owned by Derbyshire Wildlife Trust. It is one of the few remaining areas of wet grassland in the mid-Derwent

Views over the fields towards Ambergate from Whitewells Lane.

Old millworkers' cottages on Wyver Lane.

and only accessed by members. Non-members can still enjoy a good view of the wildlife as they walk along the lane.

Towards the end of Wyver Lane, a row of old millworkers' cottages with riverside gardens are a riot of colour in the summer. They look across the Derwent to the equally attractive Riverside Gardens with its flowerbeds, arboretum, bandstand, water gardens, children's playground and boating facilities.

Calder's Corner, tucked away on the western side of Belper Bridge, provides an excellent viewing point across the River Derwent towards the north and east mills, where the Strutt Family made their fortune. There is an information board and seating available.

Strutt's first two mills to be built in Belper obtained water power from a weir a short distance further up the river from Belper Bridge. As the number of mills increased, more power was needed and the distinctive-shaped Horseshoe Weir was built. It was regarded in the late 18th century as one of the most outstanding engineering structures in the country.

The arched footbridge over the road links the two sides of the former mill complex. It also had a defensive purpose, with two gun embrasures in the west walls to protect the West Mill Counting House, as at the time of the mills being built attacks by Luddites were feared.

Gardens overlooking the River Derwent on the western side of the river.

Walk Details

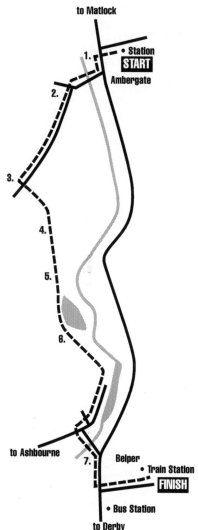

Length: 3.5 miles.

Start/Finish: Ambergate Railway Station (SK349516) – Belper Railway Station/Belper town centre.

Starting Walk: The railway station is a few yards off the A610, near to its junction with the A6 at Ambergate. There is a car park for rail users, but parking for other users is difficult at busy times and is limited to roadside parking a short distance from the station. Buses stop on the A6 on the southern side of the Hurt Arms.

Finishing Walk: Regular bus and train services are available from Belper. The bus station is on the A6, a few yards beyond King Street, and the railway station is off the same street. (See the route instructions – Point 7). To continue the walk, go to the Belper to Duffield route section.

Terrain: Mainly easy walking along quiet country lanes and access tracks, but with a short, steep climb near the beginning of the walk and a more gentle descent to Wyver Lane.

The Route

1. Leave Ambergate Station by Station Walk to reach the A610, where you turn left under the railway bridge, and then after only a few yards, go to the left along the A6, past north/south bus stops.
2. Cross the A6 to the wall overlooking Ambergate Cricket Club and where the wall ends, turn right in front of the church. Walk down the lane, cross the river bridge and turn right along a track heading for the Youth Hostel. After 30 yards go to the left to join a concessionary path, which rises up to meet Holly Lane.
3. Cross the lane and walk along Whitewells Road, a single-track road. After passing Dairywood Farm, continue for a further 100 yards to the end of a small wood, before going over a stile on your left into a field.
4. Walk down the field, keeping close to the edge of the wood, to cross another stile and continue in the same direction down the next field, heading slightly to the right towards the left-hand corner of Yewtree Wood.

Rowing near Belper River Gardens on the River Derwent.

Looking towards Belper River Gardens from the Horseshoe Weir.

5. Follow the edge of the wood down the field to arrive at a stile close to the access track leading to Lawn Cottage. Go over the stile and after a few yards join the access track, go through a stile by a metal gate and follow the obvious track as it angles to the right.

6. Continue along Wyver Lane, passing Wyver Lane Pool, to reach Belper Lane, where you bear left and then left again to cross the Derwent, past North Mill.

7. On reaching the A6, turn to the right and walk along the main road until you reach King Street and the main shopping area in the town centre. Go part way up King Street, where you will see a sign on the left for the railway station, by the side of a supermarket store. For the bus station continue a few yards further along the A6.

The bridge at Belper with East Mill in the background.

31
Belper to Duffield

The Walk

The River Derwent flows for more than 50 miles through the heart of Derbyshire. It brings with it the water power to run the mills along its valley. The dam on the right as you cross the bridge over the river at Belper at one time incorporated 12 large waterwheels, the housings of which can still be seen.

The walk soon climbs up from the river valley to join North Lane, a former Roman Road, which takes you along a ridge on the Chevin. The lane climbs very gently along the east side of Firestone Hill, along a broad, tree-lined path, which is rather uneven in places. As you walk along North Lane, there are wonderful views across the Derwent Valley and plenty of wildlife to enjoy.

At the top of Sunny Hill you can look down the narrow valley at the long rows of workers' cottages running along the hillside. Until the end of the 18th century Milford was no more than a tiny settlement, composed of a few houses near the point, about a quarter of a mile further south, where a Roman road from the Wirksworth lead mines forded the river.

The rather strange-looking tower at the top of Sunny Hill was always thought to be a sighting point to help railway workers get the line of the Milford Tunnel straight. Following recent

East Mill, Belper, built for the English Sewing Company in 1912.

House by the river passed early in the walk.

research, however, it is now thought that it was a semaphore point used to signal to drivers when the tunnel was clear.

At the bottom of the hill, Milford County Junior Mixed and Infant School was constructed on a sloping site. The upper floor that fronts onto Chevin Road was designed as a school, with the lower level used for the Strutt's wagons and carts. It is all now a school.

Although the houses and farms built by the Strutts remain largely intact, the former mills and most of the ancillary buildings have been destroyed. The foundry still remains, as does Milford Dyehouse, built two years after the death of William Strutt. The tall, round red-brick chimney dominating the site, built in the late 19th century, replaced an earlier construction.

On the east side of the river, the land rises steeply where the workers' cottages have been constructed along contours, which run parallel with the road. The terraces are unusual in that, to allow for the steep-sloping site, the east side are two storeys high and the west three. So that all the dwellings had the same accommodation, there are three east houses to every two west, even though they are back to back.

The Strutt family mansions at Milford House on Derby Road, and later at Makeney Hall, had a view over most of the workers' houses in the village. The shutters that protected nearly all the dwellings had holes drilled through them so that internal lights were clearly seen from outside. If any lights were observed still shining after 11pm, a warning would be sent to the tenants the following day about the dangers of loss of sleep.

During the latter stages of the walk there are good views across the Derwent floodplain towards Duffield. The Bridge Inn, whose gardens overlook the river, is passed when you turn right for Duffield.

Walking up the Chevin with the outskirts of Belper in the background.

North Lane a former Roman Road which takes you along a ridge on the Chevin.

Walk Details

Length: 5.5 miles.

Start/Finish: Belper town centre (SK348477)/Belper Railway Station – Duffield Village centre/Duffield Railway Station.

Starting Walk: The railway station is located off the A6, up King Street (the main shopping street in Belper), behind a supermarket part way up the street and next to the town's main pay and display car park. The bus station is a few yards away to the south, along the A6.

Finishing Walk: A regular train service is available from Duffield. The station is to the north of the village centre. Buses run from either side of the A6 at Chapel Street (southbound) and the Co-op (northbound). To continue the walk, go to the Duffield to Darley Abbey route section.

Terrain: A steady climb near the start up to North Lane, and a steep descent to Milford near the end of the route. Much of the walk is along roadside footpaths and a wide track across the Chevin. Parts of the path across the Chevin can be muddy in wet weather.

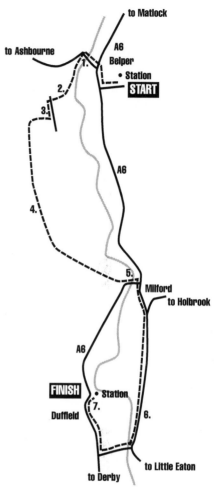

The Route

1. From the railway station and the centre of the town, walk down King Street and turn right along the A6 (the bus station is a few yards further south along the A6). Turn left at the A517 to go under the arch by North Mill. Cross Belper Bridge and immediately turn down an access road on the left to walk alongside the river.

2. Where the road ends, go through a stile and continue over two fields, with the boundary close on your left. At first keep close to the fence in the next field until it bends to the left. From this point, angle slightly towards the river and follow the Derwent for about 200 yards until, with the end of the field clearly in view, you go through a squeezer stile on the right-hand side by a metal gate.

3. Angle to the left across two fields along a well-trodden path, before following a paved path up a gulley into another field. Aim towards the corner of a fence you can see at the top of the field, cross a stile and walk past a house down to Chevin Road, where you turn left.

View back towards Belper from North Lane, with East Mill clearly seen near the centre of the picture.

4. After 200 yards, turn right at the fingerpost sign and ascend two fields, keeping close to the wall. At the top, turn left and walk along a wide track without deviating until you reach Sunny Hill, which descends steeply to Milford.

5. At the foot of the hill, turn right and then left to reach the A6 and the River Derwent, where you cross the bridge and turn right along Makeney Road.

6. Remain on the footpath alongside Makeney Road as it angles to the right, eventually dropping down to the Bridge Inn, which overlooks the Derwent.

7. Here you turn right across the bridge and follow the footpath to the A6, where you turn right again to walk through Duffield's main shopping area (where the bus stops are situated). Rail users continue past the King's Arms and over the railway bridge, before turning right for the station.

The double weir to the south of the bridge over the Derwent at Milford.

32
Belper to Duffield Circular Walk

The Walk

Belper existed before the *Domesday Book* of 1086 as a small settlement in the royal hunting forest of Duffield Frith when it was given the name of 'Beaurepaire', which means 'beautiful place'. It is now a thriving market town, but it remained a small village until the arrival of Jedidiah Strutt, who built textile mills, on land bought for him by William Slater, that transformed Belper into a prosperous town.

North Mill, the home of the Strutt's North Mill Visitor Centre, where regular guided tours are arranged of this fascinating mill, is one of the finest examples of an industrialised water-powered cotton-spinning mill that still survives in the world. The original mill on the site was destroyed by fire in 1803. Its replacement, the present mill, was built the following year by William Strutt, Jedidiah's eldest son. It is one of the best examples of an industrialised iron-framed 'fireproof' building still in existence, and is recognised as being among the most important industrial buildings in the world.

As Strutt's business grew, he needed a growing workforce, and as both Belper and Milford had small populations before his arrival, he started to build homes for his workers on land close to the mills. Long Row, which forms part of the walk, was built by Strutt in 1792–93. William

Belper Memorial Gardens during the annual Well Dressings.

Driveway to Makeney Hall a former Strutt family home, now a hotel.

Hollybush Inn at Makeney.

Street, George Street and Joseph Street, leading off Green Lane, were all named after Strutt's sons.

Duffield can be easily seen as the walk from Makeney starts to descend towards the River Derwent. Eyes Meadow stretches out across the valley floor. It holds a 48-acre sports and recreational site, the home of Duffield Cricket Club and five football pitches, plus an award-winning nature reserve. Being surrounded by the River Derwent, it is also a popular site for anglers and is home to the Derby Angling Federation.

It is thought that there may have been a settlement in Duffield, close to the junction of the rivers Derwent and Ecclesbourne, since Roman times. Roman pottery was produced at nearby Hazelwood, and the river crossing at Milford was also used in those times. Located along the A6, Duffield Hall is an imposing-looking building. It has had a substantial number of owners and was acquired as the Head Office of the Derbyshire Building Society in the 1970s, but financial problems led to its take over by the Nationwide Building Society and ultimate closure.

Chevin Golf Club, which winds its way up the hillside towards the Chevin, was opened on 13 October 1894 as a nine-hole course designed by William Lowe. Today the course covers 18 holes, with magnificent views over five counties from Chevin Ridge. The initial planning for the

The Bridge Inn where the pub garden overlooks the River Derwent.

golf course took place at Court House Farm, passed on the walk, where prisoners were once locked up to await their verdict. Nearby is the 13th hole on the course, named 'The Gibbet'; the prisoners would not have been amused.

The open countryside of the Derwent Valley provided wonderful views towards Milford and North Hill. Milford village remains almost intact, and was designated a conservation area in 1976. As you look down on the village you can see the narrowness of the valley and study the layout.

The walk along North Lane, a former Roman Road, is invigorating, with lovely views over Belper, set out like a toy town below. One unusual feature is a high wall built by the side of the lane, which at one time was used for rifle target practice.

Duffield Hall, the former home of the Derbyshire Building Society Head Office.

Walk Details

Length: 9 miles (Short Walk I – 6 miles, Short Walk II – 4 miles).

Start/Finish: North Mill, Belper (SK345481).

Starting/Finishing the Walk: Belper North Mill is on the A517 road to Ashbourne, just off the A6 between Derby and Matlock. It is next to Belper River Gardens, where there is a car park. Belper Bus Station is a short distance away to the south, along the A6, and the Railway Station is in the centre of the town, off King Street.

Terrain: Mainly country walking along paths, which are easy to follow, with some roadside walking mostly along fairly quiet roads. There are some short, moderately steep ascents and descents, but nothing particularly strenuous. It can be wet and slippery underfoot, particularly when climbing up to North Lane.

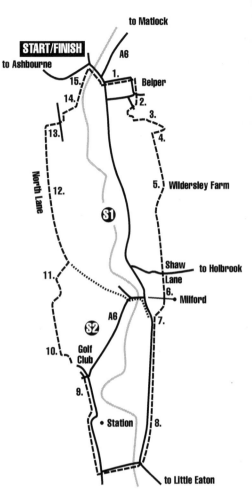

The Route

1. From Belper North Mill walk along the A517 to reach the A6, where you turn right, then left up Long Row. At the top of the road, where it narrows, turn right along Green Lane. At the end of the lane, cross King Street and walk through an archway into Belper War Memorial Park.

2. Walk through the park to the far end and turn right down New Road; just before you reach the railway bridge, turn left along Brookside. As the road dips and curves to the left, go to the right, along a path between No. 41 Brookside and several garages.

3. The path winds round first to the right and then to the left to reach Manor Road, where you turn left and then right at the top, up The Fleet. After a few yards, turn left to walk up past a sloping football pitch to reach a path at the top of the open space.

4. Turn right up the railed path and at the top of the rise continue straight ahead, soon to go through a small housing estate. On reaching Holbrook Road, turn right and walk down the road, turning left at a footpath sign where the road starts to bend to the right. Walk down Wildersley Lane.

The Kings Head on Town Street at Duffield.

5. Part way past Wildersley Farm, turn right at the Derwent Valley Heritage Way sign and walk a few yards down the field, before going to the left alongside a small area of woodland to follow the path to Shaw Lane.

6. Cross the lane and continue ahead along a fenced path to reach an open field, where you angle to the right over several fields, before turning sharp left, keeping close to the field boundary. Go straight down the next field, swinging to the right near the bottom to reach Dark Lane and walk down to Makeney village.

7. Go to the left where the lane forks past the Holly Bush public house, and turn left again at a T-junction onto Makeney Road.

Cairn at site of former Duffield Castle, which was built to protect the hunting grounds of Duffield Frith.

8. Continue along Makeney Road as it gently curves to the right and changes its name to Duffield Road to reach the bridge over the Derwent, where you turn right and then right again along the A6 to arrive at the centre of Duffield.

9. Continue along the A6 until you reach Avenue Road, on the edge of the village. Here you turn left and immediately cross the road and go down the path directly opposite, marked 'Public Footpath to Chevin'. After 25 yards the path joins the access road to Chevin Golf Club. Follow the road round, through the golf club, to reach a lane leading off to the right, where a fingerpost sign points the way.

10. Just before the lane crosses the golf course, turn left through a stile at a

North Lane a former Roman Road.

fingerpost sign and cross a field, keeping close to the field boundary. After crossing a stile, continue keeping close to the hedge before turning to the right to cross a wide bridge over a stream. Follow the obvious route uphill, with the golf course on your right.

11. The path soon curves across a field to a stile in the top corner at an intersection of paths. Continue uphill, crossing a track and continuing to climb up a short, steep slope. At the top, the route levels out to follow a fenced path by the golf course, where you go over a stile onto North Lane.

12. Here you turn left and walk along for approximately one mile, before turning right at a footpath sign by a wooden seat, a few yards prior to the lane bending to the left for Farnah Green.

13. Walk down two fields, keeping close to the wall on your left, to reach Chevin Road and turn left along the road. After 150 yards turn right opposite a fingerpost sign along the drive by the side of a house. Go over a stile and angle to the left across a field to follow a paved path through a gulley, and continue in the same direction through two further fields.

14. Go through a squeezer stile by the side of a metal gate and angle to the left towards the river, which you follow for about 200 yards towards a house standing by the river.

15. Keep to the left of the house, down the side of its boundary fence, to go through a stile. Carry straight on along a well-trodden path, keeping close to the wall on your right, to join a Severn Trent service road, which you follow to reach the A517. Turn right over the bridge to reach North Mill and the starting point of the walk.

Short Walk I

Belper Walk (6 miles)

Route (From Belper {SK345481} – Makeney – Milford – Sunny Hill – North Lane – Belper)

1. Follow the Belper to Duffield circular route instructions from Point 1 to Point 6.
2. Turn right at the end of Dark Lane into Makeney village and walk down Holly Bush Lane, turning right again at the bottom into Makeney Road.
3. Continue down the road, going to the left at the junction to join the A6. Cross the bridge over the River Derwent.
4. As the road begins to bend to the left, go up the alley on the right-hand side of the road, in front of a row of cottages.
5. Turn right along Chevin Road and then almost immediately go to the left to climb steeply up Sunny Hill, which at the top gives way to North Lane.
6. Follow the Belper to Duffield circular route instructions from Point 12 to Point 15.

Short Walk II

Duffield Walk (4 miles)

Route (From Duffield {SK345436} – Sunny Hill – Milford – Makeney – Duffield)

1. Follow the Belper to Duffield circular route instructions from Point 9 to Point 11, taking care when you reach North Lane to turn right and walk downhill, which soon becomes Sunny Hill and descends steeply into Milford.

Rifle Practice Range along North Lane.

2. Turn right at the bottom of the hill into Chevin Road, before descending a narrow alley in front of a block of cottages to reach the A6.
3. Continue in a forward direction to cross the bridge over the River Derwent and turn right up Makeney Road.
4. Walk past Makeney Hall Hotel, which is on your right, and follow the Belper to Duffield circular route instructions at Point 8, which will lead you back to Duffield.

Refreshment Stops

The Green House (Chapter 30/32) is a smart, modern Smith and Jones pub, which faces the entrance to the Memorial Gardens on King Street at Belper. (Tel. 01773 821001)

The Bridge Inn (Chapter 31/32) is a charming old pub overlooking the River Derwent on the walk from Makeney to Duffield. In the early 1800s the inn had stabling for 16 horses. (Tel. 01332 842959)

Fresh Ground Café Bar (Chapter 31/32) faces the Ritz Cinema on King Street at Belper, a few yards above the entrance to the War Memorial Gardens. The company commenced trading in 1982 and now provides a nationwide service. (Tel. 01773 828800)

Places of Interest in the Locality

Wirksworth Heritage Centre, where the 'Wirksworth Story' is told, takes you on a fascinating journey through time on three floors of the centre. The special displays are excellent, and if you want something different you can always try a computer game. (Tel. 01629 825225)

North End Mills at Wirksworth is one of the largest factory shops in the country and sells clothes for all the family. Visitors to the mills can still see hosiery being made, have a coffee and

View over Chevinside of Belper.

admire the display of old photographs of Wirksworth. Open seven days a week. (Tel. 01629 824731)

Ecclesbourne Valley Railway is based at the immaculately refurbished Wirksworth Railway Station. There is an attractive visitor centre and shop, where refreshments are served. Train rides are available on scheduled days. (Tel. 01629 823076)

St John's Chapel Heritage Centre at Belper dates back to about 1250 and contains an interesting collection of memorabilia and old photographs of Belper. Open on a limited basis. (Tel. 01773 822116)

Strutt's North Mill Visitor Centre at Belper is designed to be of interest to people of all ages. Superb displays of hand spinning wheels, Hargreaves's Spinning Jenny and many more exhibits bring this historic old mill back to life. (Tel: 01773 880474)

Belper River Gardens are tucked away at the back of North Mill and hide from the A6 behind a high brick wall. The result is that many people miss seeing these delightful gardens. Here you will find flowerbeds, an arboretum, a bandstand, water gardens, children's playground and boating facilities. (Tel. 01773 880474/841488)

33
Darley Abbey – Thomas Evans

The old village of Darley Abbey lies only two miles from the centre of Derby. It is at its most impressive when approached along either side of the River Derwent. The village itself is still full of interest since the Evans family, between 1782 and 1840, transformed it from a quiet little backwater, and it retains an important place in the industrial history of this country and now forms part of the Derwent Valley Mills World Heritage Site.

Apart from the two Evans homes, Darley House and Darley Hall, which have both been demolished, most of the houses built by the Evans family remain. The cotton mills and many of the ancillary buildings built by the Evans family survive and form the most complete 18th-century cotton mill complex in the world.

Most of the buildings are used for a varying number of light industries. The businesses are privately owned and entry into any of the buildings is not allowed without permission. There are three interpretation boards though, which can be found facing Boar's Head Mill across the weir, on a viewing platform by the car park, and at the top of New Road, near the park gates.

Few traces remain of the Augustine Abbey of St Mary, which was established at Darley Abbey in the 1140s. It subsequently became the richest and most powerful in Derbyshire, with the land and properties owned by the abbey covering an extensive area, not only in Derbyshire, but also in Nottinghamshire.

The abbey derived much of its income from large-scale sheep farming, wool production and arable farming. It was also involved in forestry and mineral extraction. The end came abruptly though, when Henry VIII ordered the Dissolution of the Monasteries in 1538. At the time the

Darley Abbey Mills, where Thomas Evans set up his cotton spinning business.

Wooden bridge by the weir at Darley Abbey.

abbey reportedly owned a hoard of pigs of lead worth several thousands of pounds. Yet wealth could not prevent the destruction of the abbey, beginning in 1538.

Most of the buildings of the once proud monastery were destroyed within two years of the passing of an Act of Parliament. The only survivors were the building in Darley Street, converted into a public house in 1980, some stonework to houses in Abbey Lane and a burial ground beneath Hill Square.

Water was the driving force and, powered by the River Derwent, an industrial hamlet sprang up at Darley Abbey. In the 1730s four mills, a paper mill, a corn mill, a fulling mill and a leather mill all existed here, every one powered by the river. But it was the decision by Thomas Evans to build a cotton mill that turned Darley Abbey into a major industrial village.

Thomas Evans was born in 1723 and educated at Trinity College, Cambridge. His family were quite well to do, acquiring a steady income primarily from their farming and mining interests at Bonsall, but it was through the entrepreneurial skills of Thomas Evans that they became very wealthy. With travel much slower in those days, Thomas Evans moved to Derby to be nearer his business interests. He expanded his interests to include a copper mill,

Darley Abbey public house with connections to the time when the monastery existed.

Hill Square Cottages, part of the first
building phase by the Evans family.

iron mill and red lead mill, as well as grinding
flint and corn, but it was the cotton mill that
was the jewel in the crown and made the
family extremely rich.

Evans lived in Derby at No. 3 St Mary's
Gate, which became the headquarters of the
Crompton and Evans Bank. This was formed
in 1771, when he entered into a partnership
with Samuel Crompton, who had been mayor
of Derby four years earlier. Crompton was a
man of considerable stature in the town and
his influence helped the bank to thrive.
Eventually Crompton tired of the business
and the bank became known as Thomas Evans
and Son, Evans's son, William, having joined
him in the business.

Both Richard Arkwright and Jedidiah
Strutt, who had gone into partnership to

Looking down Darley Park, with Little
Chester, Derby's oldest suburb, on the
other side of the Derwent.

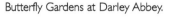

Butterfly Gardens at Darley Abbey.

build the ground-breaking mill at Cromford, were customers of the bank and for a period Evans lent money to Arkwright. The success of the two partners no doubt helped to convince Evans that he should enter the highly lucrative business of cotton spinning.

The site that Evans selected for his mill was on the eastern bank of the River Derwent at Darley Abbey. His other mills were on the opposite side of the river. For a time Arkwright was a partner in the venture, but when the mill was complete he withdrew. Evans named the mill 'The Boar's Head Cotton Mill', after the crest on the family coat of arms.

The Boar's Head trademark was used by Evans to market his thread. It achieved recognition in the many parts of the world where he traded as a symbol of quality. Awards were won at the London Exhibitions of 1861 and 1862, as well as at exhibitions in Dublin and Paris in later years.

The major part of production was the spinning of yarns for sewing cottons, knitting cottons, stockings and candlewick. The products were sold to all the main garment manufacturers in this country, as well as in Europe and North America.

Following the construction of the cotton mill in 1783, disaster struck on 4 December 1788 when the Boar's Head Mill was almost completely burned down – only the waterwheel was saved. The day after the fire, the *Derby Mercury* not only carried the story, but also printed an advertisement for skilled workmen to help rebuild the mill. Fortunately, this prompt action and the fact that the mill was insured quickly led to it being rebuilt. After the rebuilding of Long Mill, the mill works were continuously expanded well into next century.

At the outset, to ensure an adequate volume of water to drive the waterwheel and accelerate the speed with which the machinery was turned, it was necessary to increase the depth of the Derwent. The river was dredged regularly from Allestree Ford, the sediment was of good quality and the sand extracted was found suitable for building. Derby Corporation also discovered that the sand was ideal for sanding tramlines in bad weather.

As you walk through the mill complex, the route used to channel the water into the wheelhouse is indicated by the two low walls, which once formed a bridge. Other buildings on the site were used for offices, stabling and domestic purposes. A weir was constructed diagonally across the Derwent to control the flow of the river, and a bridge was built to link the village to the cotton mill. The chimney marks a later stage in the development with the arrival of steam power.

By the early 1820s, following the additions of the Middle Mill (1804–05) and the East Mill and West Mill, which were built between 1818 and 1821, the mills employed over 500 people. In addition, there were various other ancillary buildings, where reeling, dyeing and glazing took place. The long, low building on the north side of the road between the mills was the gassing shed, where stray fibres were burnt off cotton thread by passing through a gas flame at high speed.

In the mid-1800s work started at 6am during the week, the mill bell having rang three quarters of an hour previously to arouse the workers from their slumbers, with a further bell half an hour later indicating that it was time to set off for the walk to the mill. At 8.30am half an hour was taken for breakfast, and at 1pm an hour was allowed for lunch. The working day finished at 5.30pm. Saturday working was restricted to a maximum of nine hours.

All this industrial development required a substantial labour force, and the Evans family set about the task of acquiring and maintaining sufficient people to meet the growing demand for labour. This was no easy task, as many framework knitters blamed the factory system for taking away their livelihood and independence. There was also suspicion about the working conditions in factories.

Former Darley Abbey School, which was very advanced for its time when it was built by the Evans family.

Generous inducements were offered to potential workers in the form of above-average wages and new well-built brick-houses, together with a parcel of land and a cow. The houses were generally three storeys in height, the first phase of accommodation was at Flat Square, Hill Square, Brick Row and the upper part of Mile Ash Lane. About 10 years later a second phase was added in New Road and Lavender Row. This was the last major building development undertaken in Darley Abbey by the Evans family. The four houses in Mile Ash Lane, built during the early 1790s, are the oldest surviving examples of cluster houses, joined side to side and back-to-back.

At this time the vast majority of the people of working age in the village were employed by the Evans family, either at the mills or in some other capacity. It is therefore not surprising that the Evans family's sphere of influence covered most aspects of village life. In this respect they treated their workers in a much better manner than many of their contemporaries of that era.

Apart from providing houses, the Evans family had a school built in Brick Row. It was very advanced in design for its time, with spacious, airy, well-lit rooms and high ceilings. A fine clock was set in the centre of the front wall. The schoolmaster was accommodated in an apartment on the left wing of the school and the schoolmistress at the other end. It was the schoolmaster who had much the largest quarters, presumably because it was expected that he would have a family to house while his female colleague would be a spinster.

Walter Evans also had St Matthew's Church built by Moses Wood of Nottingham, with the support of a contribution from the Queen Anne's Fund, which had been set up by Act of Parliament for the construction of churches in newly built industrial areas. It was consecrated in 1819. Nine members of the Evans family are buried in the crypt. Prior to the opening of the church, for the 280 years following the dissolution of the monastery at Darley Abbey the local community had to travel to St Alkmund's in Derby for Sunday worship. The iron gates to St Matthew's are particularly impressive, one bearing the coat of arms of St Matthew and the other the Diocese of Derby, under whose authority it comes.

In front of the St Matthew's Church Fellowship Room are a large number of slate tablets identifying workers from the Evans's estate who are buried in the churchyard. It was the practice of the Evans family to pay for the burials of employees. Nearby is a stone coffin found in Darley Abbey village during excavations. The lid has been lost and its original site is not known. It has been chiselled out of a block of stone, is quite small and was possibly made for the burial of a child.

A playing field was provided for the villagers, a carnival at Whitsuntide, bathing facilities on the riverbank and a free medical service organised. Hot dinners were supplied for the old and sick in later years from Darley Hall, subject to advance notice. Burial was arranged free of charge and even an inscribed headstone.

Darley Abbey was one of the first villages in England to have its own sewage system. All the houses were painted regularly and, as the village grew, a team of painters painted each house in turn and when they were at the end of the cycle, they restarted all over again.

Thomas Evans had Darley House built in 1783, but it was demolished in the 1930s and the only building that remains is the Gate Keeper's Lodge. In 1844 the Evans family moved to Darley Hall and park, which Alderman William Woolley had built over 100 years previously.

The era ended in 1929 with the death of Ada Evans, the widow of Walter Evans. The estate was broken up and the village of Darley Abbey went into decline. The hall passed into the hands of Derby Borough Council and survived for another 33 years, before being demolished. Today, the old village of Darley Abbey is regarded as a very desirable place to live.

Thomas Evans

Born in 1723, Thomas Evans was the third child of a large family from Bonsall. His grandfather had become quite wealthy due to acquiring land through marriage that contained substantial lead deposits, and his father had continued to build up the family business interests.

Thomas moved to Derby in the mid 1740s, where he expanded the family business. In 1746 he inherited the family bank, situated at No. 3 St Mary's Gate, and four years later he married Sarah Evans, who was not related. She was the daughter of Alderman William Evans, who owned various mills in Darley Abbey.

The family banking business was extended in 1771 when Thomas entered into partnership with Samuel Crompton and formed the Crompton and Evans Bank. Both Sir Richard Arkwright and Jedidiah Strutt were customers of the bank. It later became known as Thomas Evans and Son when Samuel Crompton lost interest in the business and Evans's son joined the partnership.

By the mid-1770s Thomas had acquired the paper, corn, flint, red lead, china and leather mills, which were situated on the western side of the Derwent. Having been persuaded to go into the cotton business, he built the Boar's Head Mill, as it later became known, in 1782 on the eastern side of the river. Little is known of this mill, although evidence suggests that it was not ready for production until late in 1786 and was destroyed by fire just over a year later. It was

St Matthew's Church, Darley Abbey, where nine members of the Evans family are buried in the crypt.

quickly replaced, with sheets of tin nailed to the beams as protection. This was followed by the building of other mills and ancillary and domestic buildings.

To house their workers, Thomas Evans and his sons William and Walter ran a continuous cottage-building programme until 1830. The cottages also had yards, allotments and outbuildings provided for the benefit of their workers. St Matthew's Church and a school were built, and a playing field, free medical service, clean water, gas lighting and a sewage system were also supplied. A carnival was organised at Whitsuntide, and for those recovering from illness a convalescence home in Wales was made available.

In order to try to dissuade inhabitants of the village from getting into trouble and being unfit for work, a lock-up was built at the southern entrance to Darley Abbey. It was the watchman's duty to arrest those under the influence of drink and lock them away and to note the names of all the girls returning after 10pm. Many of the young ladies avoided this by hoisting their long skirts over their heads and running away as fast as they were able. The lock-up was demolished in 1954.

Thomas Evans appears to have been the first of the Derwent Valley Mills industrialists to have supplied the home retail market as well as other commercial concerns. He did this by supplying people's homes with sewing cottons, knitting cottons and embroidery threads and materials. He was also a prime mover in the creation of the Derby Canal, completed in 1796.

Canals were a very important factor in providing transportation for cotton. Raw cotton arrived at the ports of London, Liverpool and Hull and was transported using inland waterways to its destination. The problem was that Derby Canal did not quite reach the mill at Darley Abbey. Walter Evans was the treasurer of the Derby Canal Company and no doubt used his influence to help solve the problem. To avoid the weir at Derby, a short branch canal, called the Phoenix, was built. It had two locks, the White Bear Lock and the Phoenix Lock, which enabled the mills at Darley Abbey to be serviced.

Thomas Evans died in 1814.

34
Duffield to Darley Abbey

The Walk

There was a working corn mill on the site of the present Peckwash Mill in the 13th century. By the 17th century the mill had turned to papermaking under the ownership of Thomas Tempest, but also continued to grind corn until 1793. The mill was rebuilt, with turbines replacing waterwheels, and it became one of the biggest papermills in the country. A magnificent brick chimney was erected in 1895, but this led to a local man obtaining a permanent injunction preventing the emission of smoke from the chimney. This resulted in the business going into liquidation.

Eaton Bank, seen from the walk towards Peckwash Mill.

Quarrying was one of Little Eaton's earliest industries and, although all the quarries have now closed, there is still evidence of their workings in the hills on either side of the Bottle Brook. The quarries at Rigga Lane were still in business up to nearly 100 years ago. Riga Lane quarry can be viewed from the footbridge that spans the workings.

Peckwash Mill Chimney, which was one of the the largest papermills in the country in the 17th century.

Woodland walk approaching Little Eaton.

The driveway with the footpath running alongside at Peckwash Mill.

St Paul's Church was built in 1791, with money raised by voluntary subscription. The Lych Gate serves as a memorial to the men who fell in World War One. Their names, together with those who lost their lives in World War Two, are inscribed on plaques inside the gate. The Parish Room next door was originally the national school but is now used for local activities.

In the early 1900s Little Eaton was a popular excursion for Derby people at weekends and holiday times. The Trent bus service ran a shuttle service to the annual fair at Easter, and has been known to carry as many as 12,000 people in one day. A twopenny ride on the Derby Canal to Coxbench Wood was another highlight.

Little Eaton has expanded rapidly in recent years as a commuter village, but still retains a measure of independence with two busy industrial estates, one between the New Inn and Clock House, and the other close by the former station goods yard.

After crossing the floodplain the walk reaches Haslam's Lane, opposite the recently resited Derby Rugby Club. Further on, the route follows a toll road through Darley Abbey Mills; a charge for vehicles is currently made at set times. A large and diverse number of small businesses operate from the site.

St Paul's Church at Little Eaton, where the Lych Gate serves as a war memorial.

Walk Details

Length: 3.75 miles.

Start/Finish: Duffield town centre (SK345436)/Duffield Railway Station – Darley Abbey.

Starting Walk: The railway station is at the north end of Duffield's main street, just off the A6 along Station Approach. Buses stop in the centre of the village, Chapel Street (southbound) and the Co-op (northbound). Car parking is available in the village, also at the station for railway users only.

Finishing Walk: Walk up Old Road and turn left, local bus stops are to be found a short distance apart on either side of the road (Derby/Duffield). For buses travelling longer distances, including the Transpeak service, continue up Mile Ash Lane to the A6 and turn right for the Duffield Road stops. To continue the walk, go to the Darley Abbey to Derby route section.

Terrain: Mainly level walking along easy-to-follow paths. The final section of the walk may be flooded after particularly heavy and prolonged rainfall. In wet weather it can be muddy in places.

The Route

1. Rail users should walk up Station Approach and turn left along the A6. Continue along the main street through the village, where bus and car users should join the walk. Continue past Duffield Hall, before going left by the chapel into Makeney Road.

2. After crossing a railway bridge and the River Derwent, turn right by the Bridge Inn. At the end of the entrance to the pub car park, immediately turn right to walk down a path that runs by the side of the car park. On entering a field, turn left and keep close to the boundary on your left for two fields.

3. Keep to the path on the left of Peckwash Mill, and where this ends follow the drive to the mill up to Little Eaton Bank Road and turn right. After about 350 yards, turn sharp left up Rigga Lane and after a short distance turn right through an area of woodland.

4. Continue ahead along a well-trodden path, maintaining the same direction and keeping to the central path as it leaves and re-enters the wood. On reaching the access road to Park Farm, go to the right and walk down Vicarage Lane, past St Paul's Church, where you turn right into Church Lane. Go left on arriving at the bottom of the lane, along Duffield Road.

The Queens Head at the centre of Little Eaton.

5. At a T-junction, turn right out of Duffield Road and follow the path by a line of trees, past Derby Garden Centre and the Little Chef Restaurant. On reaching a large roundabout, go right down a lane, past Ford Farm Mobile Home Park and on arriving the end of the lane, take the path on the left and ascend a long flight of steps.

6. Go right along Derby ring road, over the railway line, and a few yards further on turn right down another long flight of steps. Follow the path round to the left and go through the tunnel under the road.

7. Walk along the access road for a few yards to the first of a series of tall marker posts, which lead you across the floodplain along the official right of way. The access road follows the edge of a series of fields round by the river and is used by some walkers to avoid any possible damage to the land, which is used to cut strips of turf.

8. At the end of the fourth field the access road leaves the side of the river at right angles and a short distance away is crossed by the footpath. Keep on the footpath and head for a stile at the end of the field. The stile is found about 35 yards from the river, to the left of a wooden fence that juts out into the field.

The tunnel under the Outer Ring Road.

9. Continue along a well-trodden path, which takes you close to the Derwent, before keeping straight on where the river bends to the right. The path soon returns to the side of the river and you walk along an access track until it bends to the right. Here you angle half left across the bottom corner of the field to go over a stile onto a rough track.

10. Follow the track to Haslam's Lane, where you turn right and walk through the Darley Mill Complex, going to the left after crossing the river to reach Mill View Gardens, which is situated at the bottom of Old Road.

The River Derwent flood plain near Darley Abbey.

35
Darley Abbey to Derby

The Walk

Few traces still exist of the abbey following the Dissolution of the Monasteries in 1538. Most of the buildings of the once-proud monastery were destroyed within two years of the passing of the Act. The only survivors were the building in Darley Street, converted into the Abbey Inn in 1979, some stonework to houses in Abbey Lane and a burial ground beneath Hill Square.

On the opposite riverbank to Darley Park is Little Chester, or Chester Green as it is more commonly known. It was once the site of a Roman town and may well have been inhabited before the Romans arrived – fragments of Iron Age pottery having been found in the area. As Derby's oldest suburb, some of its thoroughfares are also almost 2,000 years old. Today Little Chester continues to flourish and became a conservation area in 1993. The area now occupied by Darley Playing Fields was converted in the early 1900s by Derby Borough Council from the farmland estate of Ada Evans of Darley Abbey.

Situated behind Haslam's old factory on City Road at Little Chester is the fine bowstring bridge built by Andrew Handyside in 1877, which crosses the Derwent. The bridge formerly carried the Great Northern Railway's Nottingham to Derby line between North Parade and City Road, and remained in use until closed by Dr Beeching. There was a public footway along the near

Darley Abbey Mills are today used by a variety of businesses.

By the River Derwent in Darley Abbey Park.

side of the structure originally, but this was later removed when the listed bridge was renovated. Since then, pedestrians have used the main span, walking where the tracks were once laid.

St Mary's Bridge is an impressive structure of neo-classical design built by Thomas Harrison between 1789 and 1794. The original bridge pier can be viewed under the foundations of the chapel, and other remnants of the medieval bridge are to be seen in the river.

Standing on the western side of the bridge is St Mary's Bridge Chapel, one of only six bridge chapels remaining in England. It gave spiritual reassurance to travellers often about to set off on dangerous journeys. It also acted as a tollhouse, where a resident hermit collected tolls from people entering Derby. It is still used for worship and can be visited on selected days and times during the summer.

The walk through Darley Abbey Park.

Handysides Bridge formerly carried the Great Northern Railway.

Rivermead House.

The Silk Mill is an important part of the Derwent Valley World Heritage Corridor and served as Derby's Museum of Industry and History until March 2011. A short distance downstream, Exeter Bridge is a fine stone bridge built in the mid 1800s to replace an earlier wooden one. It takes its name from the Earl of Exeter, whose house stood nearby. The bridge was widened during reconstruction before World War Two.

The outbreak of World War Two delayed the completion and handover of the Council House. It was requisitioned by the RAF in 1942 and not handed back to the council for another four years. It was finally officially opened by Princess Elizabeth and her husband, Price Philip, in 1949. It is home to the city's collection of treasures, which are kept in the Mayor's Parlour.

The River Gardens, created before the building of the Council House, provide a peaceful spot away from the hustle and bustle of the city centre. The weir, missed by so many visitors to the city who tend to migrate towards the busy shopping centre, is a particularly attractive feature of the river scene.

Michael Thomas Bass, MP for Derby from 1847 to 1883, was a generous local benefactor. The grandson of the founder of the brewery that bore his name, he donated to Derby the land on which the Bass Recreation Ground now stands. Bass had purchased the three-acre site, bounded by the River Derwent and Morledge mill stream and formerly known as 'The Holmes', in 1866 to form Derby's second park. The open-air swimming baths on the site comprised of two baths, which were 100ft by 50ft and had a total of 129 dressing cubicles between them. They opened in 1873, but were destroyed after World War Two.

Boy and Ram Statue in the River Gardens.

Walk Details

Length: 2.25 miles.

Start/Finish: Millview Gardens, Darley Abbey (SK353385) – Derby City Centre/Derby Railway Station.

Starting Walk: Follow the A6 from Derby towards Duffield, then turn to the right 200 yards after the Broadway Hotel, down Mile Ash Lane. From the north follow the A6 past St Benedict's School and almost immediately turn sharp left into Mile Ash Lane. Follow the road round and, where the road dips, go to the right down Old Lane, where Millview Gardens are at the bottom, overlooking the river. There is a car park off Darley Street. There are bus stops on the A6 and along Abbey Lane for local services.

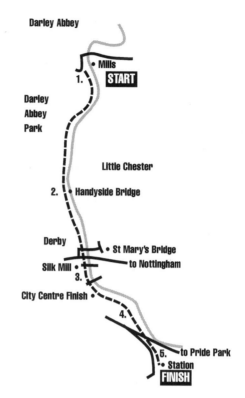

The River Gardens at Derby, with Exeter Bridge in the background.

Bass recreation ground, given to the
town by Michael Thomas Bass.

Finishing Walk: A regular train service is
available from the station, and buses run from
the forecourt back into Derby for connecting
services. The City Centre bus station is on the
Morledge, a short distance past the Council
House. To continue the walk, go to the Derby
to Borrowash Bridge route section.

Terrain: Easy, level walking through parkland and along riverside paths.

The Route
1. With Millview Gardens behind you go to the left along Darley Street. Opposite the Abbey
   Inn, turn left and cross the car park diagonally and follow the path behind the cricket
   ground to the River Derwent.
2. Continue by the riverside, passing the boathouses of both Derwent and Derby Rowing
   Clubs, to go under Handysides Bridge. Do not deviate from the riverside path, which first
   passes under St Mary's Bridge and then the bridge carrying the Derby inner ring road.
3. Pass Derby Silk Mill on the river side and continue along the path, with the recently
   renovated Cathedral Green on your right.
4. Go up a short flight of steps and cross Derwent Street with the City Centre on the right if
   you intend to leave the walk at this point. Otherwise, once over the road, go down the steps
   into the River Gardens and walk past the Council House. Continue to follow the path as it
   bends to the left and goes under a road bridge to reach the Bass Recreation Ground.
5. The path follows the river round to a T-junction of paths, where you turn to the left before
   forking to the right at a sign for Derby Railway Station.

Exeter Bridge, with the Derby Cathedral in the background.

36
Duffield to Derby Circular Walk

The Walk

A most enjoyable and absorbing walk, with so much to see and do, but beware – the section between Little Eaton and Darley Abbey is a floodplain and may be flooded after particularly heavy and prolonged rainfall.

Peckwash Mill is passed at an early stage in the walk. It is now a private house, but still retains its magnificent brick chimney, erected in 1895. There are two conservation areas in Little Eaton. The first at Eaton Bank, which includes Blue Mountain Cottages, built for workers at Peckwash Mill. The other covers three main groups of buildings in the heart of the village. Blue Mountains are named after the bluebells that carpet the surrounding woodland in spring.

The quarries have now closed, but there is still evidence of their workings in the hills on either side of the Bottle Brook. Stone from

The parish church of St Alkmund at Duffield is somewhat isolated from the village, close to the River Derwent.

Little Eaton Village Hall on Vicarage Lane.

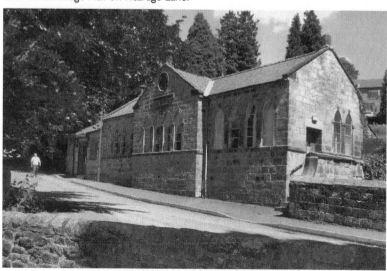

Chester Green at Little Chester,
a former Roman settlement.

Little Eaton was used in the building of Derby Cathedral, Trent Bridge at Nottingham and Birmingham Town Hall.

Little Chester, or Chester Green as it is more commonly known, was once the site of a Roman town. It may well have been inhabited before the Romans arrived – fragments of Iron Age pottery have been found in the area. As Derby's oldest suburb, some of its thoroughfares are also almost 2,000 years old. Various information boards help to tell the story.

Close by the Silk Mill is Derby Cathedral, visible from a considerable distance, which dominates the skyline with its impressive perpendicular tower. It was built early in the 16th century, but worship has taken place on this site since the 10th century. Light and spacious inside, the iron screen by Robert Bakewell is an inspirational masterpiece in this proud and beautiful building. It became a cathedral in 1927.

Abbey Lane at Darley Abbey follows on from Mile Ash Lane, where houses were built by the Evans family for their workers. Thomas Evans established cotton spinning in the village, and his mills now form part of the Derwent Valley Mills World Heritage Site. The name changes again to Church Lane at the junction with Old Lane. Much of Abbey Lane predates the Evans family's house-building era.

The River Derwent near Darley Abbey.

Slate tablets identifying workers from the Evans' Estate at Darley Abbey Church.

Little Chester Heritage Centre at St Paul's Church overlooking Chester Green.

St Matthew's Church was consecrated in 1819 and endowed by Walter Evans, as was the village school, which opened six years later. Nine members of the Evans family are buried in the crypt. In front of the St Matthew's Church Fellowship Room are a large number of slate tablets identifying workers from the Evans' estate who are buried in the churchyard. It was the practice of the family to pay for the burials of employees. A small stone coffin, chiselled out of a block of stone, is close to the slates.

It is highly probable that the Red Cow at Allestree was in existence in the early 17th century; it is shown on the 1737 map. The present building is somewhat later, the older part being late 17th century. Traditionally the pub played a major role in village life and was particularly busy when village wakes were held. The week began with the patronal festival; this was held on the first Sunday prior to the 20 November, when the death of St Edmund, the patron saint of the church, was commemorated. The wakes continued to be held until World War One. According to legend, Lord John Manners and Dorothy Vernon stopped at the Red Cow during their elopement and handed over a sum of gold in exchange for food and drink from the tavern.

Allestree Park is the wildest and most scenic of Derby's parks. A nine-hole course golf was established there in 1948 and extended to 18 holes in 1955. The lake constructed in 1825 for Sir William Evans of Allestree Hall, partly surrounded by tall trees, provides a wonderful habitat for wildlife.

The parish church of St Alkmund at Duffield stands in the water meadows of the River Derwent, a short distance from the village centre, close to the busy main Derby to London railway line. The footbridge over the line provides an excellent viewing point for trainspotting enthusiasts and interested spectators.

A small stone coffin, chiselled out of a block of stone at Darley Abbey Church.

Walk Details

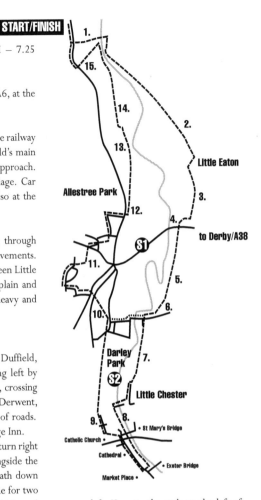

START/FINISH

Length: 11.5 miles (Short Walk I — 7.25 miles, Short Walk II — 3.25 miles).

Start/Finish: Town Street on the A6, at the centre of Duffield (SK345436).

Starting/Finishing the Walk: The railway station is at the north end of Duffield's main street, just off the A6 along Station Approach. Buses stop in the centre of the village. Car parking is available in the village, also at the station for railway users only.

Terrain: Relatively easy walking through fields, along surfaced paths and pavements. Part of the section of the walk between Little Eaton and Darley Abbey is a floodplain and may be flooded after particularly heavy and prolonged rainfall.

The Route

1. Head south along the A6 from Duffield, past Duffield Hall, before going left by the chapel into Makeney Road, crossing a railway bridge and the River Derwent, before coming to a T-junction of roads. Turn right in front of the Bridge Inn.

2. At the end of the pub car park, turn right along a footpath that runs alongside the car park. Follow the narrow path down to a field. Turn left and continue for two fields, keeping close to the field boundary on your left. Keep to the path on the left of Peckwash Mill and where this ends follow the drive to the mill up to Little Eaton Bank Road and turn right. After about 350 yards, turn sharp left up Rigga Lane and after a short distance turn right through an area of woodland.

3. Continue ahead along a well-trodden path, maintaining the same direction and keeping to the central path as it leaves and re-enters the wood. On reaching the access road to Park Farm, go to the right and walk down Vicarage Lane, past St Paul's Church. Here you turn right along Church Lane and then left at the bottom into Duffield Road. At a T-junction, go right out of Duffield Road and follow the path by a line of trees, past Derby Garden Centre and the Little Chef Restaurant.

4. On reaching a large roundabout, go right down a lane, past Ford Farm Mobile Home Park and on arriving at the end of the lane, take the path on the left and ascend a long flight of

steps. Go right along Derby ring road and over the railway line. A few yards further on turn right down another long flight of steps. Follow the path round to the left and go through the tunnel under the road.

5. Walk along the access road for a few yards to the first of a series of tall marker posts, which lead you across the floodplain along the official right of way. The access road follows the edge of a series of fields round by the river and is used by some walkers to avoid any possible damage to the land, which is used to cut strips of turf. At the end of the fourth field the access road leaves the side of the river at right angles and a short distance away is crossed by the footpath. Keep on the footpath and head for a stile at the end of the field. The stile is found about 35 yards from the river, to the left of a wooden fence that juts out into the field.

6. Continue along a well-trodden path, which takes you close to the Derwent, before keeping straight on where the river bends to the right. Shortly afterwards the path returns to the side of the river and you walk along an access track until it bends to the right. Here you angle half left across the bottom corner of the field to go over a stile onto a rough track and follow the track to Haslam's Lane, where you turn right and walk past the Derby Rugby Club entrance.

7. Turn left down Folly Road, by the side of the Rugby Club ground. Where the road ends, cross the bridge and follow the path straight down past the Community Centre. Continue forward along City Road at Little Chester, before turning right through a car park by the former Haslam factory, opposite Chester Green Road.

8. Cross Handysides Bridge and turn left to follow the riverside path without deviating, going under St Mary's Bridge to reach Exeter Bridge, where you ascend the steps and turn right by the side of the Council House.

Ancient Yew Tree in the churchyard of St Edmund's Church at Allestree.

Cottages at the top of Park Lane at Allestree.

9. At the roundabout, go to the right up Full Street, past the back of Derby Cathedral on your left and the Silk Mill on your right, continuing ahead along Sowter Road. After passing under the inner ring road, turn sharp left to walk up a path leading towards St Mary's Roman Catholic Church, at the side of which turn right up Darley Lane, which changes into North Parade. Continue straight on up Darley Grove, a rough, wide track, which later gives way to a tarmac path, to reach Darley Abbey Village at Abbey Lane, which you walk down to its junction with Old Road.

10. At this point Abbey Lane changes into Church Lane as the road gently begins to rise. Here you turn left up Darley Abbey Drive, going past the church. A soon as you have gone by the school driveway, turn right, up a tree-lined path. At the end of the path, cross Duffield Road at the pedestrian crossing and continue along Ferrers Way.

11. Take the third road on the right and walk along Cadgwith Drive, at the end of which you turn right, up Portreath Drive. Until 75 yards after passing the second turn-off for Windermere Crescent, you turn right at a cycle path sign and follow the path round to reach Allestree Recreation Ground. Leave the recreation ground at the main entrance and turn right. After 75 yards go to the left, and left again in front of the Red Cow Public House. After a few yards turn right at the footpath sign by the church and walk straight down Church Walk to the A6. Turn left, leaving the A6 at the corner with Park Lane, and continue straight ahead, down Main Avenue. At the bottom turn right and, with Allestree Park Lake on your left, follow the path round.

12. At a T-junction of paths turn right, then left along Evans Avenue and cross the busy A6. Walk down the pavement a few yards, before joining a rough track signed for Duffield. When the track ends, continue straight ahead to a stile, then angle slightly to the right over two fields

towards Fields Farm. Keep close to the fence on your right at the back of the farm, before going over a stile in the far corner into another field.

13. Follow the hedge on the left, before going over a small footbridge on the left and turning sharp right, soon to walk along the banks of the River Derwent. Continue by the Derwent until where it bends to the right. Here you follow the path in the opposite direction, through an area of woodland.

14. The path winds round the perimeter of a large field, before crossing a footbridge and heading straight across the field to the left of Peckwash Mills Chimney. Cross two more small fields, angling slightly to the left to reach a tunnel under the railway line. Turn sharp left after passing through the tunnel, keeping close to the hedge for two fields, before heading towards a stile in the centre of the next field boundary.

15. After crossing the stile walk round the right-hand edge of the field towards Duffield Church. On reaching the churchyard follow the path to the right-hand corner, go over the stile, turn left and walk up the church access road to reach Makeney Road. Turn left and walk up to the A6, where you go to the right, past Duffield Hall, to reach Town Street and the centre of the village.

Short Walk I

Darley Abbey Walk (7.25 miles)
Route (From Darley Abbey {SK353385} – Allestree – Allestree Park – Duffield – Little Eaton – Darley Abbey)

1. From Millview Gardens, which are to the right of the bridge leading to the Darley Abbey Mills complex, walk to the top of Old Road to a T-junction of roads.

2. Follow the Duffield to Derby circular route instructions from Point 10 to Point 15, but only as far as the church. Leave the church by the drive, walk up to Makeney Road and turn right and right again at the Bridge Inn. Walk past the pub and immediately follow the Duffield to Derby circular route instructions from Point 2 to Point 6.

3. Continue along Haslam's Lane and walk through the mill complex, going across the bridge over the River Derwent to reach Millview Gardens.

Short Walk II

Derby Walk (3.25 miles)
Route (City Centre {SK354364} – Darley Abbey – Little Chester – City Centre)

1. From the Tourist Information Centre in the Derby Market Place, walk to the roundabout behind the TIC and turn left up Full Street.

2. Follow the Duffield to Derby circular route instructions for Point 9.

3. Turn right down Old Road, going to the left at the bottom to cross the bridge over the River Derwent. Walk through the mill complex, watching out carefully for traffic, and continue along Haslam's Lane for a short distance to Folly Road, which is on your right.

4. Turn down Folly Road and rejoin the Duffield to Derby circular route instructions from Point 7 to Point 8.

5. After passing the side of the Council House, cross the road by the roundabout to reach the Market Place and the Tourist Information Centre.

Refreshment Stops

Abbey Inn (Chapter 34/36) is of a simple mediaeval hall layout and is thought to have been used by Darley Abbey as a guesthouse for travellers and pilgrims during the 13th century. It is located on Darley Street at Darley Abbey. (Tel. 01332 558297)

The Cathedral Coffee Shop (Chapter 35/36) is located on the ground floor of the Cathedral Centre, opposite the main entrance to Derby Cathedral. Local farm producers are the source of many of the supplies at this award-winning café. (Tel. 01332 381685)

Brunswick Inn (Chapter 35/36) is situated on the western side of the Midland Railway Station, at No.1 Railway Terrace. The inn was opened in 1842, intended for the use of railwaymen and second-class passengers. (Tel. 01332 290677)

Places of Interest in the Locality

Derby Cathedral, visible from a distance, dominates the skyline with its impressive perpendicular tower, the second highest in England to the Boston Stump. The cathedral is open on a daily basis throughout the year – the board outside gives details of services. Admission is free. The Cathedral Centre and its award-winning coffee shop are on the opposite side of the road. (Tel. 01332 341201)

St Mary's Bridge Chapel is one of only six bridge chapels left in the British Isles. It stands beside the 18th-century St Mary's Bridge, which replaced a mediaeval bridge to which the chapel was attached. The white-painted walls, the simple furniture and the lack of ostentation all add to the attraction of this wonderful place. Open on selected days during the summer. (Tel. 01332 341201)

Derby City Museum and Art Gallery houses the prestigious Joseph Wright collection of paintings. A programme of special exhibitions supports permanent displays relating to the city's archaeology, history, wildlife and local regiments. The brand new Ceramics Gallery provides an additional attraction. (Tel. 01332 716659)

Pickford's House Museum is housed in a handsome Grade I listed building, built in 1769 by Derby architect Joseph Pickford for his own occupation. It was opened as a museum in 1988 and delightfully recreates a scene of Georgian domestic life with splendidly furnished rooms and fine costume displays. (Tel. 01332 255363)

The Silk Mill – Derby's Museum of Industry and History is scheduled to close during Spring 2011 for an undefined period. The exterior of the building is of considerable historic interest.

The Quad is an £11 million purpose-built centre for art and film located in the Derby Market Place. It provides an art gallery, two cinemas, artists studios and a cafe-bar. The centre also has available spaces for local people to come and create their own artwork. (Tel. 01332 285444)

Royal Crown Derby Visitors Centre, established in 1756, now exports fine china all over the world. The Royal Crown Derby Visitor Centre, shop and restaurant facilities are open to the public daily, and factory tours are available during the week. (Tel. 01332 712800)

Little Chester Heritage Centre is located in St Paul's Church, overlooking Chester Green. For anyone interested in the local history of Derby and the Roman Empire, a visit to the Heritage Centre is essential. Information and displays also cover other important periods of history up to the present day. Open Sunday afternoons during the summer. (Tel. 01332 363354)

37
Derby Silk Mill – John Lombe

Silk is lovely to both the eye and the touch, and its production goes back to the Chinese, who jealously guarded the secret of its manufacture for 3,000 years. With those who could afford it prepared to pay a substantial price, much profitable trading for the Chinese resulted. The secret eventually emerged as a result of a deception and gradually crossed Asia and reached Europe.

At this time Italy was at the forefront of European culture, and the production of silk weaving commenced when the secret so long held safe by the Chinese was revealed. Gradually, the Italians developed the production of fine silk thread and gained a monopoly on the silk thread manufacturing process.

Demand for silk in this country was considerable, but the raw materials had to be obtained from China or Italy, making it a very expensive exercise. The weavers themselves had wooden stocking frame machines invented in 1589 by the Reverend William Lee of Calverton Nottinghamshire to help them, but it was a slow laborious and costly process.

The silk industry in this country received a considerable boost in the late 1600s, following the arrival of Huguenot refugees from France who settled in England, many of whom were skilled silk weavers. They had been driven out of their country by Louis XIV, the Catholic King of France, who opposed Protestants.

The Silk Mill was largely burnt down in 1912, but the carrying arches remain from the original mill.

In 1702 Thomas Cotchett, a middle-aged solicitor from Mickleover, became interested in the potential commercial rewards of silk thread manufacture using water-driven machinery. He entered the market and asked George Sorocold to build him a mill on an island site on the banks of the River Derwent, near the centre of Derby.

Sorocold was building himself a considerable reputation as an engineer and had recently been employed to supply Derby with piped water. He did this by pumping the water through four miles of wooden pipes from the Derwent. A wheel-powered engine was used to pump the water into a tank on the top of St Michael's Church, from where the town centre was supplied. Later Sorocold went on to install waterworks in many other towns, including Bristol, Leeds, Norwich and Sheffield.

The Silk Mill and the new Cathedral Green Bridge.

Looking across the green to Derby Cathedral, visible from a considerable distance with its impressive perpendicular tower.

The mill that Sorocold built for Cotchett, which later became known as 'The Old Shop', used 'Dutch machines', but the project was not successful. The machinery produced silk of an uneven texture and quality, and the thread created fell well short of the fine dress silk fashioned by the Italians. Disappointed and on the verge of bankruptcy, Cotchett withdrew, but the story did not end there, for John Lombe was determined that the venture would succeed at any cost.

Lombe's elder brother, Thomas, or half-brother as some historians call him, was a wealthy silk merchant and, like John, was determined to manufacture fine silk to rival that of the Italians. The problem was that the Italian method of producing silk was such a closely guarded secret that to compete without a working knowledge of the system was impossible.

Piedmont was the area in North Italy where the silk-throwing machine was first set up, which had placed the Piedmontese at the forefront of the silk industry. It was an engine that would wind, spin and twist raw silk, the finished article from which was handed to weavers or knitters to make the completed goods.

John Lombe, risking his life, went to Italy to carry out what would now be called industrial espionage. Although the ship in which he was returning was pursued by an Italian man-of-war, he arrived home safely.

The Bakewell Gates, which originally were at the entrance to the Silk Mill.

The bronze equestrian statue of Bonnie Prince Charlie on Cathedral Green.

In 1718, two years after John's return, Thomas Lombe succeeded in obtaining a patent for the three engines to be used to wind, spin and twist the silk. Shortly after that he took over Cotchett's Mill and added a much larger five-storey building. At the time that the new mill was being built, rooms were hired in various parts of Derby, including the Town Hall, in which temporary machines were installed. The machines were worked by hand and succeeded in turning out silk cheaper than the cost of imported Italian silk.

The Lombes called on George Sorocold to build the new Silk Mill, but this time his task was much greater than when he built 'The Old Shop' for Thomas Cotchett, which was to remain until the 1800s. It took him three years and cost £30,000. The complex stretched for 120 yards along the banks of the Derwent, had 468 windows and provided working space measuring approximately 40,000sq ft. It had five floors that were supported by stone arches, under which the waters from the river flowed when the Derwent was in flood. The machinery did not require a particularly strong power force, and a large undershot waterwheel was enough to meet requirements. The current to drive the wheel was supplied by the weir and tail race of the town corn mill.

The new factory was referred to as the 'Italian Works', and it was the first factory in England where all the processes were carried out under one roof utilising one source of power. It employed about 300 people and established Derby as the first industrial town in the country.

John Lombe died in 1722 after suffering from agonising pains for two or three years. Opinions vary as to his precise age, but he was certainly a relatively young man at the time of his death. Many thought that he had been poisoned by the Italians in revenge for stealing their secrets.

The Silk Mill Public House, where a mural on the wall records the Silk Trades' Lockout of 1833 and 1834.

Looking down Cathedral Green to the Silk Mill.

Plaque commemorating the Silk Trades'
Lockout of 1833 and 1834.

The patent for the 'Italian' machine was
held by Thomas Lombe for 14 years, but when
he tried to renew it in 1732 he was
unsuccessful. Because of the intense interest of
his rivals who were keen to get in on the act,
Parliament refused to renew the patent. This
would have been a terrible blow to Lombe had
he not received generous compensation. In
turn, he was required to place an accurate
model of the silk-throwing machine in the
Tower of London for inspection.

Thomas Lombe died in 1738, with 64 years
remaining on the lease of the mill. In 1739 the
lease was sold and ownership passed out of the
hands of the Lombe family. But the silk industry
in Derby continued to expand and by 1838
there were a total of 17 silk mills operating in
the town. The largest factory, in Bridge Street,
employed 750 people.

Yet life was not all straightforward for the
mill owners. In November 1833 a silk
manufacturer sacked a man who refused to pay
a fine for poor workmanship. As a result, 800
workers went on strike in support of their
colleague, and when other mill workers
followed the employers retaliated by refusing
to employ any union members. By 4 December
there were 1,300 workers on strike, and by
February there were over 2,000, while the

Engraved plaque on Exeter Bridge of
John Lombe.

owners kept the mills running with unskilled non-union labour.

Derby saw its first pickets and several men were arrested and one was given three months
imprisonment. The strike pay of seven shillings per man had run out by March and strikers began
to drift back to work. On Monday 21 April 1834 the final strikers asked to be reinstated,
although over 600 found that their services were no longer required.

The strike is recorded by a mural, which takes up the whole of one of the external walls of
the Silk Mill Public House. It was painted in 1986 and depicts the Silk Trades Lockout of
1833–34, when hundreds of newly joined trade unionists found themselves locked out because
of their membership to the Grand National Consolidated Trade Union.

The first records of the existence of the Silk Mill pub by name are dated 1874. It is likely,
however, that the pub dates back much further, to the years when Sir Thomas Lombe's historic
silk mill was fully operational. Thomas Lombe was knighted in 1727. The old inn was demolished
in 1924 and replaced on a slightly different site by the present half-timbered building.

Disaster struck in 1910 when the factory was largely burnt down, but it was rebuilt, losing two of its five storeys. Only the carrying arches and the bell tower still remained from the old mill. The tower, it would appear, only acquired its present appearance after the 1821 fire, although some of the brickwork seems to be original. Following years of declining fortunes, the building was turned into a museum, but is scheduled for closure during spring 2011 for an indefinite period. The Silk Mill is the southernmost point of the Derwent Valley Mills World Heritage Site.

The massive electric power station was once partly sited on what is now Cathedral Green. It was originally built in 1893, when electricity was starting to become a proven alternative to gas. The power station continued to increase its capacity, and in 1928 the Borough Council passed a proposal for the creation of a 'super-station'. This allowed Derby to meet all its requirements without having to buy power from elsewhere.

The location of the power atation in such a sensitive spot, so close to the cathedral and the centre of town was much criticised at the time of its construction, however. The older part of the power station was demolished in 1963–64 and a large substation constructed on the site. Following the change from coal to oil, the remaining part of the power station was demolished in the early 1970s and the site replaced by a grassed area. After remaining as a grass-covered open space for several years, the green has been redesigned to make the area more visitor friendly. An events area and a footbridge across the river have been included in the improvements.

The bronze equestrian Bonnie Prince Charlie statue on the green was presented as a gift to the city by the late Lionel Pickering, a local benefactor. It was the first equestrian statue to be created anywhere in Britain since World War Two and celebrates the 250th anniversary of the invasion of 1745. Following the arrival of Bonnie Prince Charlie and his Jacobite army in Derby on 4 December 1745, an important decision in British history was made. On the previous day the Prince had been advised by his generals to withdraw and return to Scotland. They were not happy being so far into enemy territory without the expected support of the English Jacobites, and doubtful that the planned French invasion to support the venture would take place. The decision to withdraw was made against the wishes of the Prince, who wanted to continue. London was in panic, and had the march continued, the path of British history could well have been changed.

John Lombe

In the early 15th century, the Lombe family came to prominence in Norfolk as wool importers. They were also involved in the weaving of worsted and silk and John Lombe, who was born at Norwich in the late 1600s, took a close interest in machines from an early age. In his teens he was able to understand and make suggestions for the improvement of spinning machines. His chance to put his knowledge of mechanics to good use came after the engineer, John Sorocold, built the first Silk Mill on an island site in the River Derwent for Thomas Cotchett.

At the age of 20 he came to Derby and was involved with Cotchett in trying to find a way of producing a fine silk of consistent quality. Unfortunately, despite all their best efforts the venture was unsuccessful and Cotchett close to bankruptcy admitted failure and withdrew. However, Lombe, who was much younger than Cotchett, refused to throw in the towel and was intent on finding a solution whatever the risks.

View from Exeter Bridge of the Silk Mill.

The Italians had the monopoly in the efficient production of fine silk of consistent good quality and because of this were able to charge a high price for the finished article. They closely guarded the secret of their success and would have continued to have maintained a stranglehold on the market had it not been for the initiative of John Lombe.

In order to obtain the secrets from the Italians, he first of all set about learning the language and bringing his knowledge of mathematical drawing up to date. Then with the financial support of his brother Thomas, he travelled to Piedmont in Italy, where the silk was produced and after bribing two Italian workers, he gained access to the resource. He inspected the machinery and made copious notes and drawings, placing each drawing in a bale of raw silk bound for Derby, via his brother's London agents.

However, just after he had completed the plan, the Italians began to realise what was going on. His life was in great danger, for had he been caught and found guilty, the penalty was to be hung from a gibbet by one foot until he was dead. Fortunately a ship was just leaving the dock and he was able to escape. An Italian man of war, dispatched by the furious Italians, gave chase but it was outpaced and three weeks later John Lombe arrived back in Derby, his mission successfully completed.

Thomas Lombe obtained a patent for the new machine, which was constructed as a result of the Italy trip and silk of fine quality started to be produced. A factory was built by George Sorocold to enable the Lombe's to mass produce silk on a large scale. It was the first factory in England where all the processes were carried out under one roof and utilising one source of power. It employed about 300 people and established Derby as the first industrial town in the country.

John Lombe died on the 16 March 1722, in very mysterious circumstances, after living in agony for two or three years. It was widely thought that he had been slowly poisoned by an Italian woman whom he had possibly first met while working in Italy. She had arrived in this country in 1718 and quickly obtained employment at the mill. It was from this point that Lombe's health began to steadily deteriorate and he suffered intense abdominal pains before eventually dying. The theory was that she had been sent from Italy to exact revenge for the loss of their silk monopoly. This led to her arrest, but the case could not be proved and she was deported.

He was buried at the old St Peter's Church, but it was demolished a year later and rebuilt and all trace of his tombstone has been lost. There is an engraved plaque in his honour on Exeter Bridge. His brother is also remembered by the arms that appear on Robert Bakewell's wrought iron gate made for the Silk Mill entrance, which in recent times has been repositioned near its original location.

38
Derby to Borrowash Bridge

The Walk

Derby has played an influential role in the railway industry for more than 170 years. The station was one of the first to open in the country and has always held a very important position in the rail network. In the early 1980s British Rail decided to replace it with a modern station. The coats of arms of the Midland Railway and the City of Derby were put on the new frontage.

In order to meet the requirements of travellers, the Midland Hotel was built to a high standard for the use of first-class travellers. It was the first purpose-built railway hotel in the country. The Brunswick Railway and Commercial Inn opened in 1842, intended for the use of railwaymen and second-class passengers.

Derby Railway Works played an influential part in the railway industry for more than 170 years.

The historic Roundhouse at Derby Station, superbly restored by Derby College.

Rest and viewing area by the River Derwent.

Ten years after the arrival of the railway, the Railway Institute was founded as a reading room for Midland Railway employees. The present building dates back to 1892, when the decision was made to remove several houses to accommodate the new cultural centre for railway workers. At one time this contained a library of over 14,000 books. In addition, there were several other rooms set on one side for recreation, as well as reading, including a lecture and concert hall, billiards room, classrooms and a coffee room.

Pathside funiture along Riverside Walk at Pride Park.

The Roundhouse site, with its storage sheds and historic locomotive turntable, had been deteriorating since it was, for the most part, vacated in 1990. The city council took over the site in 1994, when only the offices under the clock tower were occupied and the rest of the site was in a dilapidated state. This was recognised by English Heritage, who listed it the same year, along with the complex of listed buildings, in their Buildings at Risk Register. After several plans to save it had failed, this historic site is once again something that all Derby people can look on with great pride following Derby College's superb restoration.

Gravel is now extracted at the former Chaddesden Railway Sidings.

The Meadows, situated on the other side of the river from Pride Park, was originally farmland. But with the arrival of the railway in 1839, the land was taken over by the railway industry and became known as Chaddesden Sidings. In recent years sand and gravel has been extracted from the site for the building industry.

Pride Park was formerly the site of Derby's railway manufacturing industry. It has now been very successfully turned into a home for a large number of industrial and commercial units. Derby County's impressive football stadium proudly forms the centrepiece of the development whose name it bears. The stadium was opened by HM the Queen on 18 July 1997. Unfortunately, the first League match at the stadium, against Wimbledon FC, ended in embarrassment when the match had to be abandoned due to floodlight failure. Representative football came to Pride Park for the first time in February 1999 when England Under-21s played the French Under-21s team. This was followed in May 2001 by a full international match, England versus Mexico, played in front of what was a record crowd for the stadium at the time.

At the rear of the park and ride car park on Pride Park is 'The Sanctuary', a bird and wildlife reserve. It was formerly a gas works tip and had long been protected from development as part of the 'green wedge' policy of Derby City Council. It was not until 2001, however, that the importance and potential of this site was fully appreciated, when the work to create the Pride Park business site came to a close. The site has deliberately been kept quite bare and devoid of trees, which attracts birds like the skylark, meadow pipit, the common tern and many other species.

After passing under the bridge that connects Pride Park with the Wyvern Centre is one of the 1,000 mileposts that mark the creation of the National Cycle Network. Alvaston Park is a public open space, backing onto the River Derwent, with a five-acre lake. The former Wilmorton College (Derby College) site on the western side of the park has been converted into a housing development.

Soon after this point the river meanders back and forth and creates a sizeable island, where a nature reserve has been established. Further along the river, Spondon Sluices was built as a form of flood protection after a disastrous flood in Derby in 1932.

Derwent Flood Barrier.

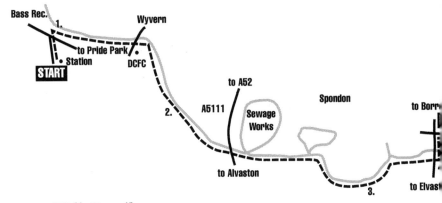

Walk Details

Length: 4.25 miles.

Start/Finish: Derby City Centre (SK354364)/Derby Railway Station–Borrowash Bridge.

Starting Walk: For those starting from the city centre, the route instructions from Point 1 should be followed. The railway station is well signed from the city centre. There are several car parks between the city centre and the railway station, as well as a railway car park. A bus service operates between the bus and railway stations.

Finishing Walk: Walk up Station Road from Borrowash Bridge to the road intersection, where bus stops can be found on the Derby/Nottingham road. Eastbound passengers should turn right, and westbound passengers to the left. To continue the walk, go to the Borrowash Bridge to Shardlow route section.

Terrain: Easy, level walking all the way along the riverside path.

The Route

1. From the Market Place in Derby City Centre, walk towards Exeter Bridge, but before crossing the river, turn right and follow the path through the Riverside Gardens at the rear of the Council House. Go under the road bridge and round Bass Recreation Ground turning left at a T-junction and heading towards Pride Park. From Derby Railway Station walk to the right along Railway Terrace, cross the road opposite the Alexandra Public House and turn right at a sign for Riverside Walk. Descend a flight of steps and turn right to walk along the side of the River Derwent towards Pride Park.

2. Continue on the riverside path through the industrial estate, passing under the bridge that connects Pride Park with the Wyvern Centre to reach Alvaston Park.

3. The route continues alongside the river, going under a road bridge, all the time keeping close to the river and passing the Derwent Flood Barrier and a footpath that leads round to Elvaston Castle.

Weir on the River
Derwent.

4. From this point the path
follows an embankment
at the end of which the
path forks slightly to the
right. Soon the road
linking Borrowash and
Elvaston is reached,
where you turn left (take
the stile on the right just
before the river if you
wish to do the next
section of the walk from
Borrowash Bridge to
Shardlow) and walk up
Station Road to
Borrowash.

The Wilmot Arms on
Derby Road at
Borrowash.

39
Borrowash to Shardlow

The Walk

After following an embankment by the river, several fields are crossed to reach Ambaston, a tiny, very quiet village. There is no church, shop or pub and the houses are ribbon built along the Main Street. A play area has been provided for the children, in what must rank as one of the quietest villages in the county, which can only be reached by road via two meandering lanes from Elvaston and Shardlow.

The start of the walk at Borrowash Bridge by the Elvaston to Borrowash road.

Shardlow has two parts: to the west is the old village which predates the eastern side, which sprang up with the construction of the Trent and Mersey Canal. It is the western side of the village that the walk first visits, where you pass The Dog and Duck, standing at the crossroad of the road to Aston-on-Trent, which is one of the oldest buildings in the

Walkers near the River Derwent during the early part of the walk.

The River Derwent.

The Malt Shovel Public House is located on the wharf at Shardlow.

village. On the other side of the road, the walk passes the impressive stone-faced Shardlow Hall, which dates from 1684 and was built for Leonard Forsbrooke, the man who was instrumental in the emergence of Shardlow as an inland port. Today it is one of the best-preserved inland canal ports in the country.

A walk along the canal towpath brings you into contact with many of the old buildings of the Canal Age, including the massive warehouses that once stored ale, cheese, coal, cotton, iron, lead, malt, pottery and salt; and the wharves where goods were loaded and unloaded. The buildings are mostly now used for different purposes, but are still largely intact. This is where the skilled craftsmen worked: the boatbuilders and repairers, the chandlers, rope-makers and blacksmiths.

An attractive feature along the canal bank are the restored iron mileposts that mark every mile to Preston Brook, near Runcorn, the northern end of the canal. The New Inn and The Malt Shovel, once the house of the manager of the attached malt warehouse, are popular canal-side pubs.

The coming of the railways in the mid-1800s brought a decline in Shardlow's prosperity. But the growth of the leisure boat industry in recent years has once again returned Shardlow to its former vibrancy, with the splendid new marina and boatbuilders' yard, completed in 1975, always busy with boats.

Boats by the canal bank at Shardlow, one of the best-preserved inland canal ports in the country.

Approaching Derwent Mouth Lock.

After passing under the bridge carrying the road to Great Wilne, the walk continues along the canal towpath. It was James Brindley from Derbyshire, who could not read or write properly but had a brilliant brain, who designed the canal. The Trent and Mersey Canal, known as the Grand Trunk, was Brindley's most celebrated enterprise. It connected canal systems throughout the country, and after it opened Shardlow became an important inland port.

The River Derwent flows into the River Trent a short distance on from Derwent Mouth Lock. Until 2002 the walk could continue over Long Horse Bridge, but the bridge was removed on safety grounds and at the time of writing has not been replaced.

Derwent Mouth Lock, close to the point where the Derwent flows into the Trent.

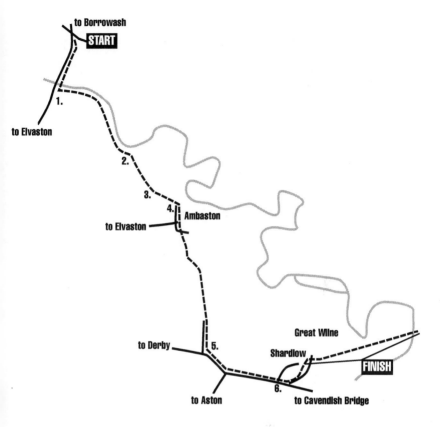

Walk Details

Length: 4.75 miles.

Start/Finish: Borrowash Bridge (SK414338) – Shardlow and Derwent Mouth.

Starting Walk: Borrowash is on the A6005 Derby to Nottingham Road, with the B5010–Station Road leading off to the south, near the main shopping area. There is a regular bus service from Derby to the centre of Borrowash. Street parking is available in Station Road and the roads nearby.

Finishing Walk: From London Road Bridge (see route – Point 6) go to the left along London Road for bus stops to Derby, Loughborough and Leicester. There are buses back to Borrowash from Derby.

Terrain: Level walking at first along the riverbank, then through fields and down a quiet lane to Shardlow. The final section takes you along the towpath of the Trent and Mersey Canal.

243

The meeting point of the River Derwent and the Trent and Mersey Canal.

The Route

1. From the centre of Borrowash walk down Station Road and immediately after crossing the bridge over the River Derwent*, turn left at the footpath sign and descend a flight of steps to go over a stile at the bottom. (*The bridge is the point reached in the previous walk).

2. Continue close to the river, soon walking along a flood-prevention embankment, and passing through two stiles before the embankment ends. After a short distance a narrow strip of recently planted trees is reached. Here you should keep a careful lookout for a short flight of steps on your right, which you descend to enter an open field.

3. Go half left and follow the path through a gap in the hedge into the next field. Maintain the same direction to a stile about 15 yards to the right of the bottom corner of the field. Continue bearing slightly to the left to go over a stile to the right of a gateway at the bottom of the field.

4. Keep close to the hedge for about 50 yards and then cross a stile on your left. Head across the field, aiming towards a house you can see in the distance, to reach another embankment, where you keep straight on before turning left down an access road.

5. After only a few yards you go over a stile by a metal gate, turning right out of the access road and walk down Main Street, Ambaston. Continue straight on out of the village, taking good care all the time, down a quiet country lane for about 1.5 miles to reach Shardlow.

6. Go left along London Road and follow the footpath round. After about 0.75 miles cross the bridge over the canal and immediately turn left to reach the canal bank, which you follow for a further mile to Derwent Mouth. At this point turn round and walk back to Shardlow, before leaving the canal at the London Road Bridge.

40
Elvaston to Ambaston Circular Walk

The Walk

After leaving the main vehicular entrance to Elvaston Castle the walk takes you along a tree-lined route round the northern edge of the castle grounds. This area of the park is used to stage events, including the County Show and Elvaston Steam Rally. Home Farm, just out of view on the walk, near the north-western corner of the woodland, is scheduled to be the location of a golf clubhouse. The country park has over 200 acres of woodland, parkland and formal gardens and is the home of the Elvaston Local Nature Reserve.

The clock tower at Elvaston Castle.

At the heart of the park is Elvaston Castle. Repair costs to the castle and rising running expenditure have led Derbyshire County Council to say that they can no longer fund all the requirements. This has led to strong opposition, but plans are currently in hand for the castle to be turned into a hotel.

The earliest recorded settlers in the parish were the Saxons, but they were not the first to live in the area. Gravel workings near the neighbouring village of Shardlow have revealed Iron Age artefacts. At the time of the Domesday Survey, all that was recorded for Elvaston was a church, corn mill, blacksmith's shop and 52 acres of land.

Fisherman by the River Derwent.

Following the Norman Conquest the estate passed through the hands of several families. In the early 16th century, however, it was acquired by the Stanhope family, in whose ownership it remained for nearly 400 years. During the Civil War, the Stanhopes, a staunch Royalist family, found themselves sandwiched between Derby and Nottingham, who both supported the Parliamentarians. As a result, the house and gardens were ransacked by soldiers searching for arms.

The present-day gothic-style castle was designed in the early 19th century by the architect James Wyatt for the 3rd Earl of Harrington. The Earl also wanted 'Capability' Brown to landscape his 200-acre estate, but Brown declined, saying, 'The place is so flat and there is

Stile near Ambaston.

The main street in Ambaston.

such a want of capability in it.' Following the death of the 3rd Earl, his son gave the task to William Barron, a 25-year-old Scot who had trained at the Botanical Gardens in Edinburgh and was looking to establish a reputation as a landscape gardener.

The first problem Barron had to deal with was the waterlogged ground, which he solved by having drainage ditches. It was only after five years that the soil was finally ready for planting. The Earl was becoming impatient to see results and Barron planted fully grown trees, keeping them alive and healthy by transporting them vertically, with their branches outstretched and their root balls intact.

Elvaston Village Hall, built in 1852 and previously used as a Church of England School.

To the north of the castle Barron created an ornamental lake with islands and rockery. On the southern side he developed half a

Elvaston Cricket Club's smart new ground.

Elvaston Castle was the home of the Stanhope family for nearly 400 years.

dozen formal gardens. In order to compensate for the lack of an interesting view, he enclosed the gardens with high hedges to shape a view within the gardens themselves. For contrast he designed two striking open avenues, 50ft wide and 400 yards in length.

By 1850 Barron had planted examples of every species of European conifer then known, 11 miles of yews, a yew tunnel, a pinetum, a kitchen garden and a lime avenue leading from London Road to the Golden Gates. The elaborate blue-and-gold cast-iron gates were acquired by the Earl as a 'spoil of war', having reputedly been taken from the Royal Palace at Madrid to Versailles then to Elvaston.

Until after the death of the 4th Earl the gardens remained a private place, but his brother, who succeeded him in 1851, opened the gardens to the public. Despite having to pay a high admission price for those days, thousands of people visited, often travelling considerable distances.

The estate remained under the control of the Harrington family until 1939, after which the house was used for a short period of time as a teacher training college. It was then left vacant until 1969, when it was established as the first country park in England.

After leaving the castle and gardens behind, the nature reserve in the grounds of the country park is soon passed. Here are to be found several pools and observation hides. A short distance further on the impressive Borrowash Weir is seen, before the walk follows a route close to the river to Borrowash Bridge. After following an embankment by the river, several fields are crossed to reach Ambaston, a tiny, quiet hamlet. There is no church, shop or pub and the houses are ribbon built along Main Street. It can be reached by narrow lanes both from Shardlow and Elvaston.

St Bartholomew's Church with its fine perpendicular tower.

There are number of interesting buildings in Elvaston, including the Village Hall, which was built in 1852 and previously used as a Church of England School. The Clockhouse, a three-storeyed building built as a 'Refuge for the Aged Poor' is now a retirement home. The former vicarage, Thurlaston Grange, is an attractive listed building dating from the Georgian period.

Close to the castle is St Bartholomew's Church with its fine perpendicular west tower. Marks can still be seen on Sir John Stanhope's tomb, made by the Roundheads' swords. Only a short distance from the church is Elvaston Cricket Club's impressive tree-lined ground and new pavilion. The club played at Lords for the first time in 1994, when they won the National Village Cup. They have made rapid strides in recent years and are now one of the leading teams in the county.

The film *Women in Love* created a lot of local interest at the time of its production. Elvaston Castle was used for interior (fight) and exterior (drowning) scenes.

A rockwork feature in the gardens at Elvaston Castle.

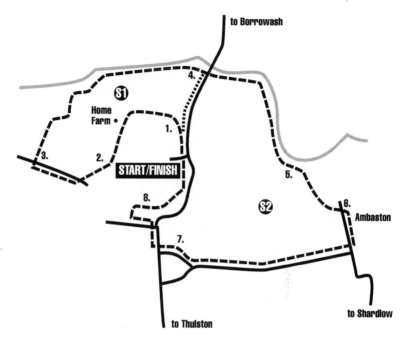

Walk Details

Length: 5.5 miles (Short Walk I – 2.5 miles, Short Walk II – 3.25 miles). There is also the opportunity available to walk around Elvaston Castle's magnificent gardens.

Start/Finish: Elvaston Castle car park (SK413332).

Starting/Finishing the Walk: Located to the south-east of Derby and can be accessed from Borrowash in the north and from the Alvaston to Shardlow road in the south. The best service for bus users is that to Borrowash, where passengers should alight and follow Station Road down to the main vehicular access to Elvaston Castle, a distance of approximately one mile. Trains do not stop at Borrowash. Returning bus passengers should walk back to Borrowash up Station Road to the road intersection, where bus stops can be found on the Derby/Nottingham road. Eastbound passengers should turn right and westbound passengers to the left.

Terrain: Good level walking, with surfaced and grassed paths and a quiet walk along the lane from Ambaston to Elvaston.

The Route

1. Walk back towards the car park entrance and 25 yards before reaching the road, turn left down a wide, tree-lined gravel path. Continue straight on at an intersection of tracks, and soon after this point the track starts to curve to the left.

2. Ignore all the paths to the left and continue along the same track as it bends back towards Elvaston Castle. On reaching another intersection of paths, maintain the same direction to cross a bridge over the upper end of Elvaston Lake.

3. After a short distance the clock tower at Elvaston Castle comes into view on the left. At a T-junction of routes, turn to the right along a tarmac access road. The road soon bends to the left, where after a few yards take the track to the right, marked 'National Cycle Network'.

4. Continue straight on towards Alvaston and on reaching an intersection of tracks, just before reaching East Lodge, turn right, marked 'Riverside Path'. This takes you past Elvaston Castle Nature Reserve. Follow the track round and turn right to follow a raised embankment close to the river. As you near Borrowash Bridge, the path bends slightly to the right to reach the Borrowash to Elvaston Road.

5. Cross the road to the stile opposite and descend a flight of steps to go over a stile at the bottom. Continue close to the river, soon walking along a flood-prevention embankment and passing through two stiles before the embankment ends. After a short distance, a narrow strip of recently planted trees is reached. Here you should keep a careful lookout for a short flight of steps on your right, which you descend to enter an open field. As you will appreciate from the warning, the steps are easy to miss.

6. Go half left and follow the path through a gap in the hedge into the next field. Maintain the same direction to a stile about 15 yards to the right of the bottom corner of the field. Continue bearing slightly to the left to go over a stile to the right of a gateway at the bottom of the field. Keep close to the hedge for about 50 yards and then cross a stile on your left. Head across the field, aiming towards a house you can see in the distance, to reach another embankment, where you keep straight on before turning left down an access road.

7. After only a few yards you go over a stile by a metal gate, turning right out of the access road to reach Main Street at Ambaston. Walk down the street and at the edge of Ambaston village turn right along a quiet country lane, heading towards Elvaston. In just under a mile take a right-hand fork in the lane, which soon leads to Elvaston village. Here you turn right and after a short distance take a left turn marked for 'Elvaston Cricket Club and the Village Hall'.

8. Walk along the lane past the village hall, and a short distance before reaching the Golden Gates, turn right along an estate road marked for 'Elvaston Castle'. Follow the road round, past the Old English Garden, before arriving back at the vehicular entrance to Elvaston Castle. Here you turn left and return to the starting point of the walk.

Short Walk I

Elvaston Walk (2.5 miles)
Route (Elvaston Castle {SK413332} – Elvaston Castle Nature Reserve – Borrowash Bridge – Elvaston Castle)

1. Follow the Elvaston to Ambaston circular route instructions from Point 1 to Point 4.

2. Turn right to walk down the pavement of the Borrowash to Elvaston road for approximately 300 yards.

3. After passing a cottage, turn right, and in another 35 yards go to the left down a wide gravel path to return to the vehicular entrance to Elvaston Castle.

4. Turn right to return to the starting point of the walk.

Short Walk II

Ambaston Walk (3.25 miles)

Route (Elvaston {SK413332} – Borrowash Bridge – Ambaston – Elvaston)

1. Follow the Elvaston to Ambaston circular route instructions for Point 1, but only as far as the intersection, where you turn right to reach the Borrowash to Elvaston road.
2. Turn left and walk up the road towards Borrowash Bridge. Turn right just before reaching the bridge and follow the Elvaston to Ambaston circular route instructions from Point 5 to Point 8.

Refreshment Stops

Wilmot Arms (Chapter 38) is a cosy little pub situated on Derby Road at Borrowash, a short distance to the west of Station Road. It has been refurbished recently, but still retains much of its former appeal. (Tel. 01332 663636)

Harrington Tea Rooms (Chapter 38/40) is located in Elvaston Castle. Seats are available both inside and in the courtyard. If, as expected, Elvaston Castle changes ownership in the future, the current arrangements are likely to be discontinued. (Tel. 01332 752592)

The Harrington Arms (Chapter 38/40) is situated at Thulston, a short distance to the south of Elvaston. It is a traditional village pub, serving fresh, home-cooked food. (Tel. 01332 571798)

The Malt Shovel (Chapter 39) located at The Wharf in Shardlow is a comfortable canal-side pub with an open fire and olde worlde atmosphere. Seating is available outside overlooking the Trent and Mersey Canal. (Tel. 01332 799763)

Places of Interest in the Locality

Pride Park Football Stadium is the home of Derby County Football Club and it provides behind-the-scenes tours of the stadium, which will impress the visitor whether they are a football fan or not. Please telephone for bookings and full tour details. (Tel. 0870 444 1884)

The Sanctuary at the rear of the Park-and-Ride car park on Pride Park is a bird and wildlife reserve. Access is not possible onto the Sanctuary itself. All main features can be easily viewed from a number of points around the perimeter fencing, all accessible from the car park. This is currently open Monday–Saturday 7am to 7pm, but closed on Sundays and for Derby County home matches.

Elvaston Castle Country Park was the first country park to be opened in Britain. Set in 200 acres of parkland with an ornamental lake, extensive gardens, stoney grottoes, rock archways and many other interesting features. Open daily. (Tel. 01332 571342)

Shardlow Heritage Centre is an interesting place to visit. It is housed in the Old Salt Warehouse and features displays of canal and village life of this historic inland port. Normally open at weekends and Bank Holidays from Easter to the end of October. Shardlow is one of the best-preserved inland canal ports in the country. It is a fascinating place to explore, still busy with boats, now used for leisure and not for commerce. (Tel. 01332 793368/792334)

41
Shardlow – James Brindley

Shardlow is one of the best-preserved inland canal ports in the country. It is a fascinating place to explore, still busy with boats, now used for leisure and not for commerce. The boats range from traditional narrowboats with brightly painted liveries, frequently bedecked with pretty boxes filled with flowers in summer, to pleasure craft of all shapes and sizes.

All this activity is good news for the canal-side pubs, which swarm with customers in the summer and at weekends. A walk along the canal towpath brings you into contact with many of the old buildings of the Canal Age, including the massive warehouses that once stored ale, cheese, coal, cotton, iron, lead, malt, pottery and salt; and the wharves where goods were loaded and unloaded. The building are nostly now used for different purposes, but are still largely intact. This is where the skilled craftsmen worked: the boatbuilders and repairers, the chandlers, rope-makers and blacksmiths.

Waterway traffic has always been important to the village as it was originally a river port. Rivers had regularly been used for transport and the River Trent is navigable as far as the Humber Estuary. In the second half of the 17th century the Wilden Ferry, near Shardlow, became the head of the Trent navigation. This part of the Trent was leased from the Cokes of Melbourne Hall by the Forsbrooke family. They tried to monopolise river traffic between the

The Clock Warehouse was originally used as a transfer point for canal boats and river barges.

Iron mileposts mark every mile along the canal from Shardlow to Preston Brook.

ferry and Nottingham and were so successful that Shardlow Hall was built out of the profits. In 1760 the ferry was replaced by Cavendish Bridge, on the Derbyshire side of which is a toll board listing charges, ranging from two shillings and sixpence for coaches to a halfpenny for soldiers.

The use of river transport goes back much further than the days of the Wilden Ferry. In 1999 a 12ft-long oak boat was exposed by spring floods at Shardlow quarry in the bed of a former side channel of the River Trent. The boat, probably dating from the middle Bronze Age, *c.*1300 BC, was still carrying some of its cargo of quarried stone. Archaeologists examining the find described its discovery as 'spectacular'. A small remnant of the boat and other details of this discovery are available for inspection at the Heritage Centre.

The rapid growth of industry in the second part of the 18th century required an improved and inexpensive

The Old Salt Warehouse on the western side of London Bridge.

The London Road Bridge over the Trent and Mersey Canal.

Canal boat passing through Shardlow on route for the River Trent.

transportation system if it was to be sustained. Much of the development was inland, so the coastal route was usually out of the question. Rivers, often obstructed by weirs and fish pools, rarely could be used for long-distance haulage. Roads had been improved by the growth of turnpikes, but were not suitable for moving large volumes of goods. Packhorses were still relied on in Derbyshire to transport goods – slowly and laboriously. The time was ripe for a new form of effective transportation of heavy goods.

A solution came when the Duke of Bridgewater, who was looking for an economical method of transporting coal from Worsley to Manchester, turned to James Brindley for help. He had previously consulted other engineers who had been unable to find a way of crossing the River Irwell. Brindley's proposal to build an aqueduct over the river was greeted with scorn by his contemporaries, but the Duke backed his judgement and financed the project. This proved to be a wise decision, and when the work was completed the price of coal sold in Manchester halved, but the Duke's wealth substantially increased due to improved sales.

Brindley also built a canal to link Manchester to Liverpool for the Duke of Bridgewater. The canal era was now in full swing and the seemingly tireless Brindley travelled hundreds of miles on horseback surveying the countryside for new routes along which to build his inland waterways. His most ambitious assignment was the construction of the Trent and Mersey Canal, known as the Grand Trunk, which linked Liverpool, Bristol and Hull. It connected canal systems throughout the country, and after it opened Shardlow became an important inland port.

The rapid transportation expansion led to Shardlow's population growing from 200 in 1780 to over 1,300 in 1841. The coming of the railways in the mid-1800s brought a decline in Shardlow's prosperity; no longer was the canal busy with long-distance haulage. The warehouses were put to other uses and the area began to decay. A limited amount of canal trade continued until the 1950s, when the last delivery of grain was made. The growth of the leisure boat industry in recent years has once again returned Shardlow to its former vibrancy, with the splendid new marina and boatbuilders yard, completed in 1975, always busy with boats.

Industrial buildings are now recognised as a fundamental part of our heritage and Derbyshire is fortunate to have such an important survivor of the Canal Age within its boundaries. In 1974 the port area of Shardlow was designated a conservation area, which has led to the preservation of the port. The only other inland canal port that has been conserved in near its original state is at Stourbridge.

The Clock Warehouse, combining a pub and restaurant, is a spectacular restoration from its original use as a transfer place from river barges to canal boats. It was built in 1780 for the storage of goods, prior to them being transferred to a narrowboat, as river barges could not navigate the 7ft-wide locks beyond Burton upon Trent. The main London to Manchester road, which passed through the village, was also used to redistribute goods. Opposite, in the oldest canal warehouse in the village, is Shardlow Heritage Centre, where the fascinating story of the village is told.

On the main A6 The Navigation Inn once served river traffic. Broughton House belonged to one of the rich merchants, John Sutton, although he never lived there. It is said that he had it built to spoil the view of his business rivals, the Soresby family, who lived at The Lady in Grey, formerly known as The Lodge.

An attractive feature along the canal bank are the restored iron mileposts that mark every mile to Preston Brook, near Runcorn, at the northern end of the canal. The Malt Shovel, once the house of the manager of the attached malt warehouse, is a popular canal-side pub. By the village green is a row of interesting old canal workers' cottages.

Swans enjoying a swim on the Trent and Mersey Canal.

The village is made up of two distinct parts: to the west is the old village, which predates the canal port, while to the east is the inland port created when the Trent and Mersey Canal was constructed. St James Church was built on the western side of the village in 1839 on land donated by the Sutton family of Shardlow Hall, which stands opposite. Worshippers previously had to travel by packet boat to Aston-on-Trent. Shardlow Hall was built between 1680–84 and it seems surprising at first that only the back of the Hall can be seen from the road; originally it faced the road that ran from the Wilne Ferry to the Dog and Duck, thought to be one of the oldest buildings in the village.

James Brindley

Born in 1716 at Tunstead, a hamlet in the parish of Wormhill, near Buxton, James Brindley's father was a farm labourer. He was an idle man who spent his money on drink and gambling and was not able to afford an education for his son. James spent much of his childhood walking round the fields rattling a tin can to scare off the birds.

When James was older he drove wagons to the local corn mill, where he watched corn being ground by the use of water power. The process fascinated him and at the age of 17 he was apprenticed to a millwright, where he was given the chance to mend machinery and showed extraordinary mechanical skills. This led to him being sent all over the country to repair machines.

After setting up his own business at Leek, which quickly expanded, James was nicknamed 'The Schemer' because of his remarkable ability to find solutions to mechanical problems. Despite his brilliant brain, he never learned to read or write properly. This did not stop the Duke of Bridgewater approaching him, however, to find an economical way of transporting coal from the Duke's estate at Worsley to Manchester. Brindley astounded other engineers who had been unsuccessful at finding an answer to the problem and who laughed at his ultimately successful proposal.

He did this by building an aqueduct over the River Irwell. It stood on three great stone arches, 17ft up, with a towpath alongside the canal for the horses to pull the boats the 900 yards to the other side of the river. Sightseers flocked to see for themselves if what they had heard was true. They gazed in awe as they witnessed horses pulling one barge after another across the great chasm. This was the beginning of the canal system in this country and Brindley's name, like his canals, spread far and wide.

Brindley's most celebrated enterprise was the Trent and Mersey Canal, known as the Grand Trunk. It took 11 years to build and linked Liverpool, Bristol and Hull, connecting up with other canal systems throughout the country. After it opened Shardlow became an important inland port and the port is well preserved to this day.

The efforts of this remarkable man are perhaps best summed up in the words of a contemporary historian, who said, 'He has chained seas together…his ships do visibly float over valleys. The Mersey and the Thames, the Humber and the Severn have shaken hands.' Brindley died on the 27 September 1772 at the age of 56, after a short illness brought on as a result of getting drenched in a heavy downfall of rain while surveying a canal near Leek. He was so dedicated to his work that he carried on with his task without changing his clothes and became ill as a result.

Printed in Great Britain
by Amazon